SMP 16–19

Mechanics 2

Moments, energy and circular motion

CAMBRIDGE
UNIVERSITY PRESS

Much of this book is based on earlier SMP books to which the following people contributed.

Chris Belsom	Paul Roder
Stan Dolan	Tom Roper
Judith Galsworthy	Mike Savage
Andy Hall	Bernard Taylor
Mike Hall	Carole Tyler
Janet Jagger	Nigel Webb
Ann Kitchen	Julian Williams
Melissa Rodd	Phil Wood

PUBLISHED BY THE PRESS SYNDICATE OF THE UNIVERSITY OF CAMBRIDGE
The Pitt Building, Trumpington Street, Cambridge, United Kingdom

CAMBRIDGE UNIVERSITY PRESS
The Edinburgh Building, Cambridge, CB2 2RU, UK
40 West 20th Street, New York, NY 10011–4211, USA
477 Williamstown Road, Port Melbourne, VIC 3207, Australia
Ruiz de Alarcón 13, 28014 Madrid, Spain
Dock House, The Waterfront, Cape Town 8001, South Africa

http://www.cambridge.org

First published 2002

Printed in the United Kingdom at the University Press, Cambridge

Typeface Minion and Officina   *System* QuarkXpress®

A catalogue record for this book is available from the British Library

ISBN 0 521 78801 3 paperback

Cover photograph: Powerstock Zefa

Contents

Using this book   iv

1 Work and kinetic energy   **1**

A   Speed and distance   1
B   Potential energy   4
C   Conserving energy   6

2 Momentum and energy   **12**

A   Collisions   12
B   Perfectly elastic collisions   14
C   Newton's law of restitution   16

3 Circular motion   **20**

A   Angular speed   20
B   Acceleration   23
C   Gravity   26

4 Centres of mass   **31**

A   Moments   31
B   Centre of gravity   35
C   Centre of mass   38
D   Applications   43

5 Variable forces in one dimension   **47**

A   Impulse   47
B   Work done by a variable force   51
C   Springs and elastic strings   55
D   Elastic potential energy   57

6 Modelling circular motion   **60**

A   Motion in a horizontal circle   60
B   Motion in a vertical circle   64

7 Energy transfer   **68**

A   Elastic potential energy   68
B   Work and energy   72
C   Power   75

8 Impulse and work in two dimensions   **78**

A   Constant forces   78
B   Variable forces   82

Answers   **87**

Index   **108**

Using this book

Most sections within a chapter consist of work developing new ideas followed by an exercise for practice in using those ideas.

Within the development sections, some questions and activities are labelled with a **D**, for example **2D**, and are enclosed in a box. These involve issues that are worth exploring through discussion – either teacher-led discussion in the whole class or discussion by students in small groups, who may then feed back their conclusions to the whole class.

Questions labelled **E** are more demanding.

This book builds directly on the foundations laid in *Mechanics 1*. There the relations between **displacement**, **velocity** and **acceleration** are central. For constant acceleration there are formulae embodying the connections. When acceleration varies with time, differentiation and integration may be required.

Some sections of both books are concerned with one-dimensional motion. In two dimensions, vector ideas are essential and acceleration need not be in the direction of motion. An example of the latter occurs in projectile motion.

The concept of **momentum** introduced the idea of **force** (equal to the rate of change of momentum). For constant force, the change in momentum equals force × time, the **impulse**.

Newton's three laws link forces with motion. Especially important is the second law in the form

$$\mathbf{F} = m\mathbf{a}.$$

You will need these formulae:

Constant acceleration
$$\mathbf{v} = \mathbf{u} + \mathbf{a}t$$
$$\mathbf{s} = \mathbf{u}t + \tfrac{1}{2}\mathbf{a}t^2, \quad \mathbf{s} = \mathbf{v}t - \tfrac{1}{2}\mathbf{a}t^2$$
$$\mathbf{s} = \tfrac{1}{2}(\mathbf{u} + \mathbf{v})t, \quad v^2 = u^2 + 2as$$

General motion
$$\mathbf{v} = \frac{d\mathbf{r}}{dt} \text{ and } \mathbf{a} = \frac{d\mathbf{v}}{dt}$$

Momentum
$$\text{Momentum} = m\mathbf{v}$$

Forces
$$\text{Resultant force} = m\mathbf{a}$$
$$\text{Weight} = m\mathbf{g}$$

1 Work and kinetic energy

A Speed and distance (answers p. 87)

When investigating a car crash, police and insurance claim investigators need to know at what speed the crashed vehicle was travelling before the brakes were applied. The length of time taken for skidding cannot be measured but the distance of the skid is often easy to measure.

In the questions that follow, take $g = 10$ m s^{-2}.

1 A series of skid tests is carried out in which a car skids to rest with its wheels locked by the brakes. The table below shows the lengths of skid marks, x metres, for various speeds, u km h^{-1}.

u	0	40	60	80	100
x	0	9	20	36	56

What would you expect the length of the skid marks to be for an initial speed of 120 km h^{-1}? Find x in terms of u.

2 (a) A diver steps off a springboard which is 5 m above the surface of a swimming pool. Find how fast he is moving when he hits the water.
  (b) The diver in (a) springs upwards with an initial speed of 7.5 m s^{-1}. How high above the board will he be when he comes to instantaneous rest? What will be his final speed when he hits the water?
  (c) What will be his final speed if he is thrown off the springboard with an initial speed vertically downwards of 7.5 m s^{-1}?

3 The diver of question 2 has an initial upward speed of u m s^{-1} off a springboard height h m above the water. If his final speed on hitting the water is v m s^{-1}, find an expression for v^2 in terms of u, g and h. Would your answer have been different if the initial speed u m s^{-1} had been downwards?

4 An object of mass m is accelerated in a straight line by a constant force F, from speed u to speed v. Its (t, v) graph is as shown.

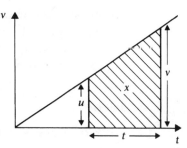

Use the constant acceleration formulae and $F = ma$ to obtain the expression

$$Fx = \tfrac{1}{2}mv^2 - \tfrac{1}{2}mu^2$$

for the product, force × distance.

5 Comment on your answer to question 1 in the light of question 4.

The concept of 'force × distance' is as useful as that of 'force × time' which you have used previously. The expenditure of energy involved in pushing something along for some distance has come to be known as 'doing work'. To be more precise, Fx is known by engineers, physicists and mathematicians as the **work done** by the force.

The energy of motion acquired by the object as a result of being pushed (and having 'work' done on it) is represented by $\frac{1}{2}mv^2$. This form of energy is called **kinetic energy**, from the Greek word for motion, κινεσις (kinesis). Other forms of energy will be introduced later in this chapter.

> For a constant force accelerating an object in a straight line,
> $$Fx = \tfrac{1}{2}mv^2 - \tfrac{1}{2}mu^2$$
> Work done = Change in kinetic energy

The units of energy are known as **joules** (abbreviated to J). These are named after James Prescott Joule (1818–89), an English physicist who established that the various forms of energy known at that time – mechanical, electrical and heat – are basically equivalent. Each can be transformed into any of the others.

1 N m (from force × distance) is the same as 1 joule.
Also, 1 kg m^2 s^{-2} (from $\frac{1}{2}$ mass × speed^2) is the same as 1 joule.

6 Name some forms of energy, other than mechanical, electrical and heat. List some ways in which one form is transformed into another.

Example 1

(a) A sports car of mass 1000 kg is travelling at 50 m s^{-1}. What is the work done by the frictional forces which bring it to rest?
(b) If it is brought to rest in 50 metres, what is the total retarding force (assumed to be constant)?

Solution

(a) Work done = change in kinetic energy
$$= \tfrac{1}{2}mv^2 - \tfrac{1}{2}mu^2 = \tfrac{1}{2} \times 1000 \times 0^2 - \tfrac{1}{2} \times 1000 \times 50^2$$
$$= -1\,250\,000 \text{ joules}$$

(b) Let the total retarding force be F newtons.
   Work done $= F \times 50 = -1\,250\,000$
   $\Rightarrow \quad F = -25\,000$ newtons

Note that the force is negative because it acts in the opposite direction to the direction of the motion. A general extension of the work and energy equation to cases where the force and motion are not in the same direction requires a vectorial treatment. This will be considered later.

Example 2

A car hits a telegraph pole head-on. There are skid marks of length 27 metres, and it is established from analysis of the impact damage that the car must have been travelling at 55 km h^{-1} on impact. A skid test shows that, in similar circumstances, from the speed of 70 km h^{-1}, the car would have been expected to stop in 25 metres. At what speed was the car travelling when the brakes were applied?

Solution

Speeds in km h^{-1} must be converted to speeds in m s^{-1}. In this case,

$$70 \text{ km h}^{-1} \approx 19.5 \text{ m s}^{-1} \qquad \text{and} \qquad 55 \text{ km h}^{-1} \approx 15.3 \text{ m s}^{-1}$$

For the skid test, let F be the resultant force on the car.

$$F \times 25 = \tfrac{1}{2}m \times 0^2 - \tfrac{1}{2}m \times 19.5^2 \Rightarrow \frac{F}{m} = -7.6$$

For the pre-collision skid,

$$F \times 27 = \tfrac{1}{2}m \times 15.3^2 - \tfrac{1}{2}mu^2$$

$$\Rightarrow \quad \frac{F}{m} \times 27 = \tfrac{1}{2} \times 15.3^2 - \tfrac{1}{2}u^2$$

$$\Rightarrow \quad -7.6 \times 27 = \tfrac{1}{2} \times 15.3^2 - \tfrac{1}{2}u^2$$

$$\Rightarrow \quad u = 25.4$$

When the brakes were applied, the car was travelling at about 25 m s^{-1} (about 56 mph).

Exercise A (answers p. 87)

1 A car of mass 1500 kg is travelling at 40 m s^{-1}. Considering this motion only, and neglecting any energy associated with rotation of moving parts of the car, how much kinetic energy does the car possess? Give your answer in joules.

   If the car's brakes are applied, locking the wheels and causing the car to skid to a halt in 100 metres, what is the average retarding force due to friction between the tyres and the road?

2 A bullet of mass 15 grams passes horizontally through a piece of wood 2 cm thick. If its speed is reduced from 500 m s^{-1} to 300 m s^{-1}, find the average resistive force exerted by the wood.

3 A car of mass 1 tonne accelerates with a constant acceleration from 0 to 108 km h^{-1} in 15 seconds. Find the net forward force on the car. If the engine is then switched off and the car is allowed to come to rest under the action of a resistive force of 500 newtons, find the total distance travelled by the car.

4 A car of mass 800 kg is capable of producing a net force of 3100 newtons in first gear, 2000 newtons in second gear, 1500 newtons in third gear and 1100 newtons in top gear. Find the speed attained if the car is driven from rest for 10 metres in first, 20 metres in second, 30 metres in third and 40 metres in top gear.

5 A van of mass 2250 kg hit a low obstruction which caused it to turn on its side and slide 32 metres before hitting a barrier. Impact tests suggest that it hit the barrier at 50 km h^{-1}. Tests involving towing the remains of the van, on its side, on the same road surface in similar conditions, suggest that the friction forces retarding the sliding van amount to about 2×10^4 newtons. At approximately what speed did the van start to slide on its side?

6 Find the kinetic energy of the Earth due to its motion around the Sun. (You may assume the mass of the Earth to be 6.04×10^{24} kg, the mean radius of its orbit to be 1.5×10^8 km and the length of the year to be 365 days.)

7 A sledge of mass 240 kg is pulled on level ground from rest by dogs with a total forward force of 150 N against a resistance of 45 N. How fast will the sledge be moving after it has gone 56 m?

8 The braking efficiency of a car is defined to be the percentage of the car's weight that the brakes can supply as a resistance to motion. Find how far a car travels whilst being slowed:

   (a) from 100 km h^{-1} to 50 km h^{-1} by brakes that are 75% efficient;

   (b) from 80 km h^{-1} to a standstill by brakes that are only 40% efficient.

9 A toboggan of mass 5 kg slides from rest down an incline of 1 in 6. After travelling 80 m it has acquired a speed of 10 m s^{-1}. Find the resistance, assumed constant.

B Potential energy (answers p. 88)

Lift a pencil vertically through a height h. When you release the pencil above the table it does not remain stationary. It falls down because gravity is still acting on it. The pencil held at rest above the table has zero kinetic energy, but it can acquire kinetic energy because gravity has the potential to do positive work on it as it falls to the table. For this reason, the pencil is said to have **gravitational potential energy** (PE) *before* it falls.

> ● The gravitational potential energy (PE) of a body is always measured relative to an arbitrary fixed reference position where its value is taken to be zero. It is defined as the work that would be done by gravity if the body were to move from its present position to the fixed reference position.
> ● A particle of mass m kg, at height h metres above the floor, has gravitational potential energy mgh joules relative to the floor.
>
>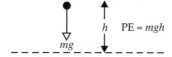
>
> ● If you raise a mass m kg a distance h metres in a vertical direction, you increase the gravitational potential energy by mgh joules, where g is the gravitational force per unit mass.

Example 3

Calculate the gravitational potential energy, relative to the ground, of a 2 kg mass at a height of 3 metres above the ground.

Solution

$PE = mgh = 2 \times 10 \times 3$
$= 60$ joules

Note that the mass has this potential energy whether or not it is allowed to fall.

Example 4

A child of mass 20 kg is sitting at the top of a slide of length 4 metres which is inclined at 25° to the horizontal. Find her gravitational potential energy relative to B. (Take $g = 10$ m s^{-2}.)

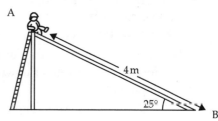

Solution

The child's height above B is 4 sin 25° metres.
So her PE $= 20g \times (4 \sin 25°)$
$= 338$ joules

Exercise B (answers p. 88)

Take $g = 10$ m s^{-2}.

1 Calculate the gravitational potential energy, relative to the ground, of a particle of mass 5 kg if it is 2 metres above the ground.

2 Calculate the gravitational potential energy, relative to the ground, of a child of mass 30 kg sitting at the top of a slide of length 5 metres and inclined at 36° to the horizontal.

3 A circus performer of mass 70 kg swings on a rope of length 8 metres.

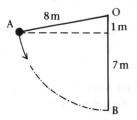

Calculate the change in his potential energy as he moves from A to B.

4 (a) Calculate the work done by gravity (to the nearest joule) when a 50 kg hod of bricks is carried up a ramp which has length l and is inclined at an angle θ to the horizontal if

   (i) $l = 34.4$ metres, $\theta = 5°$ (ii) $l = 8.0$ metres, $\theta = 22°$

   (b) Explain why the increase in the gravitational potential energy of the bricks is approximately the same for each of the ramps.

5 A bricklayer carries a hod of bricks (50 kg) up a ladder. Calculate the length of the ladder if it is inclined at 70° to the horizontal and the increase in the gravitational PE of the bricks is 4300 J.

C Conserving energy (answers p. 88)

1 A swimmer of mass 70 kg slides into a swimming pool down a straight chute inclined at an angle θ to the horizontal. Draw a diagram to show the forces acting on the swimmer.

   (a) If air resistance and friction are ignored, what is the resultant force on the swimmer down the chute? What is his acceleration?

   (b) If the top of the chute is a distance h m above the water surface, find the length of the chute. If the initial speed of the swimmer is u ms^{-1} and his speed on entering the water is v ms^{-1}, find an expression for v^2 in terms of u, g and h.
   Show that $\frac{1}{2}mv^2 - \frac{1}{2}mu^2 = mgh$.

(c) Did the value of θ affect v^2 in (b)? Would your answer have been the same if frictional forces had been taken into account?

(d) If the chute had been curved and did not reach right down to the water, would the value of v^2 in (b) have been the same?

2 (a) A ski-jump consists of three parts. The slopes AB, BC and CD are at angles 70°, 60° and 80° respectively to the vertical. B is 5 m lower than A, C is 10 m lower than B, and D is 2 m lower than C. If the speed of a skier at A is zero, use your answer to question 1 to find the speed of the skier at D. (You may neglect friction, air resistance and 'bump' effects at B and C.)

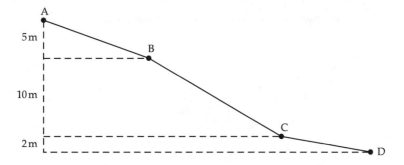

(b) What would be the final speed of a skier at the foot of the ski-jump shown below?

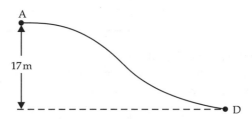

In these questions, the change in kinetic energy (KE) is equal to the change in potential energy (PE); when one is lost, the other is gained. This will always be true when no forces other than gravity do work.

A constant force does no work if the direction of its line of action is perpendicular to the displacement of its point of application.

An example is the normal contact force on a straight slide.

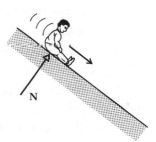

A force with variable direction does no work if the object on which it acts has a variable velocity which changes direction in such a way that the direction of the line of application of the force is always perpendicular to the velocity of the object.

An example is the normal contact force on a curved slide.

Example 5

A marble rolls down a chute and becomes a projectile.

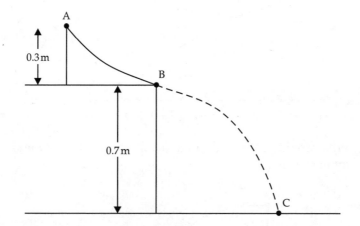

(a) Calculate its speed at B and at C.
(b) If it is moving at 20° to the horizontal at B, find the horizontal and vertical components of the velocity at C.

Solution

Assume that the marble is a particle of mass m kg and that there is no friction.

(a) The normal contact force does no work.

So gain of KE = loss of PE

For the motion from A to B, $\frac{1}{2}mv^2 = mg \times 0.3$
$$v = 2.45$$

For the motion from A to C, $\frac{1}{2}mv^2 = mg \times 1$
$$v = 4.47$$

The speed is 2.45 m s^{-1} at B and 4.47 m s^{-1} at C.

(b) At B, the horizontal velocity component $= 2.45 \cos 20°$
$$= 2.30 \text{ m s}^{-1}$$

At C, the horizontal velocity component $= 2.30 \text{ m s}^{-1}$ also;

the vertical component $= \sqrt{4.47^2 - 2.30^2}$
$$= 3.83 \text{ m s}^{-1}$$

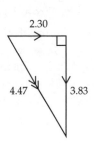

Exercise C (answers p. 88)

Take $g = 10 \text{ m s}^{-2}$.

1 A squash ball of mass 20 grams is hit vertically upwards with speed
   15 m s^{-1}.
   (a) What is its potential energy relative to its initial position when it
       has travelled 3 metres?
   (b) What is its speed at that point?
   (c) What is its potential energy at the highest point of its path?

2 A bob of mass 100 grams, on a string of length 1 metre, is
   released from rest when the string makes an angle of 80° with
   the vertical as shown. What is its speed at the lowest point of
   its path?

3 Two ball bearings (one twice as heavy as the
   other) can swing freely on the ends of light
   strings as shown in the diagram.

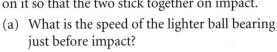

   The lighter ball bearing swings down and collides
   with the heavier one, which has a piece of putty
   on it so that the two stick together on impact.

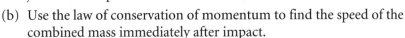

   (a) What is the speed of the lighter ball bearing
       just before impact?
   (b) Use the law of conservation of momentum to find the speed of the
       combined mass immediately after impact.
   (c) Predict the angle of swing of the combined mass.

4 A child of mass 30 kg slides down a helter-skelter sitting on a mat.
   If the child's speed at the bottom is 4 m s^{-1} and the height of the
   helter-skelter is 10 m, find the loss of PE, the gain of KE and the work
   done by friction.

5 A girl (mass 40 kg) swings on the end of a 5 metre rope in
   a gymnasium. If she initially jumped at 3 m s^{-1} off a horse
   2 metres high on a level 4 metres below the point of
   suspension of the rope, which was taut, find

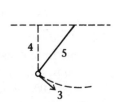

   (a) her maximum speed
   (b) her maximum height above the ground.
   (c) Did you need to know her mass?

6   A Scout sets up an aerial runway starting
    from 10 metres up a tree.

    (a) If the lowest point is 2 metres off the
        ground, at what speed will someone
        using the runway pass that point?
        (State clearly what assumptions you
        make.)

    (b) If the end of the aerial runway is
        4 metres off the ground, with what
        speed will someone reach this point?

    (c) Do you think such a runway would
        be safe?

7   A ski-jumper of mass 75 kg is practising on a dry ski slope. He travels
    35 metres down a slope inclined at 55° to the vertical. Find his speed
    then, if 90% of the potential energy lost is converted into kinetic energy.

8   A sledge of mass 10 kg slides 25 metres down a slope. If the potential
    energy lost is 500 joules, what is the angle of elevation of the slope?

9   A girl of mass 50 kg walks 100 metres up a slope of 30° to the
    horizontal. What is the potential energy gained? What is the source of
    this energy?

10 A boy and his bicycle have a total mass of 60 kg. He is travelling at
    6 m s^{-1} at the top of a hill and at 10 m s^{-1} when he reaches the bottom,
    having dropped a (vertical) distance of 30 m.
    Find

    (a) the loss of potential energy

    (b) the gain of kinetic energy

    (c) the work done by the brakes.

    Comment on the assumptions made.

11 A body of mass 3.1 kg is projected up a 20° slope at 4.2 m s^{-1}. It stops
    after 1.6 m.
    Find

    (a) the kinetic energy lost

    (b) the potential energy gained

    (c) the work done by friction

    (d) the friction force

    (e) the coefficient of friction.

12 A car of mass 650 kg (including the occupants) accelerates up a 1 in 10
    hill for a distance of 150 m. The speed increases from 18 m s^{-1} to
    30 m s^{-1}. Find the work done by the engine assuming 90% efficiency
    (i.e. 10% of the work is used to overcome friction and air resistance).

13E   A projectile of mass m has initial velocity $\begin{bmatrix} a \\ b \end{bmatrix}$ and initial speed U. It

starts at the origin and after time t, its height is h and its speed V.

Express U, V, h in terms of a, b, t and hence show that

$$\tfrac{1}{2}mV^2 = \tfrac{1}{2}mU^2 - mgh$$

After working through this chapter you should

1   know that for a constant force accelerating an object in a straight line,
$$Fx = \tfrac{1}{2}mv^2 - \tfrac{1}{2}mu^2$$
work done = change in kinetic energy

2   know that the standard unit for work or energy is the joule

3   know that forces at right angles to the velocity do no work

4   know that gravitational potential energy relative to an arbitrary level is mgh joules, where h is the height above the chosen level

5   know that one form of energy may be turned into another form, e.g. potential energy into kinetic energy.

2 Momentum and energy

A Collisions (answers p. 90)

1D You can hear the impact when two snooker balls collide. This means that sound energy has been created. What must be the source of this energy?

You saw in *Mechanics 1* that momentum is conserved in a collision.

2D A body P of mass 6 kg, moving at 5 m s^{-1}, collides with a body Q moving in the same straight line in the same direction.

Q has mass 4 kg and speed 2 m s^{-1}.

(a) Calculate the total momentum of the two bodies and their total kinetic energy before they collide.

(b) After the collision, P moves at 3 m s^{-1} in the same direction as before. Find the speed of Q then and the new total kinetic energy.

You should have found in question 2 that a little mechanical energy is lost. It will have been converted into other forms of energy like sound and heat.

Example 1

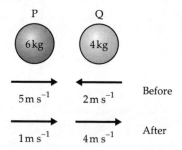

P   Q

6kg   4kg

5m s^{-1} 2m s^{-1} Before

1m s^{-1} 4m s^{-1} After

The diagram represents a head-on collision of the bodies in question 1. Show that momentum is conserved and find the loss of KE.

Solution

Momentum before $= 6 \times 5 - 4 \times 2 = 22$ kg m s^{-1}

Remember that momentum is a vector quantity; the numbers must be subtracted since the bodies are moving in opposite directions.

KE before $= \frac{1}{2} \times 6 \times 5^2 + \frac{1}{2} \times 4 \times 2^2 = 83$ J

The KE of a moving body is independent of its direction; the numbers must be added.

Momentum after = $6 + 16 = 22$ kg m s^{-1} = momentum before.

Momentum is conserved in a collision, so the data given are plausible.

KE after = $\frac{1}{2} \times 6 \times 1^2 + \frac{1}{2} \times 4 \times 4^2 = 35$ J
KE lost = $83 - 35 = 48$ J

More than half the kinetic energy has been lost in this more dramatic collision.

> KE is lost whenever two bodies collide.
> In an explosion, KE is gained.

Calculation of the momentum and kinetic energy of a body both require its mass and velocity. But the concepts are quite different; momentum is a vector while kinetic energy is not. We say kinetic energy is a *scalar* quantity. In two dimensions, applying conservation of momentum requires vector methods (drawing or using components).

In a collision, momentum is conserved but KE is lost. When a car goes round a bend at a steady speed, momentum is changed but KE is not.

Exercise A (answers p.90)

1 A Dodgems car of mass 120 kg, moving at 3 m s^{-1} with its power switched off, hits another car of mass 140 kg directly from behind. The second car was originally at rest, and moves forward after the collision at 2 m s^{-1}. Find the subsequent speed of the first car and the loss of KE.

2 A descent module, mass 400 kg, is docking with its command module, mass 1200 kg. Before they come together they are both moving at constant speed in the same direction, the command module at 4 m s^{-1} and the descent module at 5 m s^{-1}. Find the speed of the recombined spaceship after docking and the loss of KE.

3 In a game of bowls, one wood of mass 0.9 kg hits a stationary jack. Its speed is reduced from 2 m s^{-1} to 1.5 m s^{-1}. The whole motion takes place in the same line and the jack moves off at 3.2 m s^{-1}; what is its mass? Find the loss of KE.

4 Two punts collide head-on. The total mass of punt A, including passengers, is 500 kg, and that of B is 300 kg. Before the collision A was moving at 0.75 m s^{-1} and B at 0.5 m s^{-1} in the opposite direction. After the collision B rebounds at 0.5 m s^{-1}. How fast and in which direction does A travel afterwards? Find the loss of KE.

5   A shell, mass 6 kg, is travelling horizontally at 400 m s^{-1} when it breaks into two fragments, masses 4 kg and 2 kg, which continue to travel in the same horizontal plane. The 4 kg mass moves off at 500 m s^{-1} at 30° to the original direction. Find from a momentum vector diagram, or by calculation, the speed and direction of the other fragment. Find the gain in KE.

6   A satellite of mass 200 kg is attached to a nose-cone of mass 12.5 kg. When travelling at 9600 m s^{-1} the two are separated by an internal impulse of 1.6×10^5 N s in a direction at right angles to the line of flight. Find the subsequent speeds of the satellite and nose-cone and the deflection of each from the original line of flight. Find also the gain in KE.

7   Two billiard balls, A and B, both of mass 0.1 kg, collide. A is moving at 2.5 m s^{-1} and B at 2 m s^{-1} at 120° to the direction of A's velocity. A is deflected through 80° by the collision and B is then moving perpendicular to it. Find by drawing or calculation, the momenta of A and B after the collision. Deduce the final speeds and the loss of KE.

B   Perfectly elastic collisions (answers p. 90)

For the next two sections, we will deal only with motion in a straight line.

It is useful to consider an idealised collision in which there is no loss of kinetic energy. Such a (fictional) event is called a **perfectly elastic collision**.

Consider the following collision where both kinetic energy and momentum are conserved.

Speed of approach $= u_1 - u_2$ Speed of separation $= v_2 - v_1$

$$\boxed{m_1} \mapsto u_1 \quad \boxed{m_2} \mapsto u_2 \qquad \boxed{m_1} \mapsto v_1 \quad \boxed{m_2} \mapsto v_2$$

Kinetic energy: $\frac{1}{2}m_1 u_1^2 + \frac{1}{2}m_2 u_2^2 = \frac{1}{2}m_1 v_1^2 + \frac{1}{2}m_2 v_2^2$

Momentum: $m_1 u_1 + m_2 u_2 = m_1 v_1 + m_2 v_2$

$\Rightarrow$ $m_1(u_1^2 - v_1^2) = m_2(v_2^2 - u_2^2)$ and $m_1(u_1 - v_1) = m_2(v_2 - u_2)$

$\Rightarrow$ $\dfrac{m_1(u_1^2 - v_1^2)}{m_1(u_1 - v_1)} = \dfrac{m_2(v_2^2 - u_2^2)}{m_2(v_2 - u_2)}$

$\Rightarrow$ $\dfrac{(u_1 - v_1)(u_1 + v_1)}{(u_1 - v_1)} = \dfrac{(v_2 - u_2)(v_2 + u_2)}{(v_2 - u_2)}$

$\Rightarrow$ $u_1 + v_1 = v_2 + u_2$

$\Rightarrow$ $u_1 - u_2 = v_2 - v_1$

This result shows that the speed of separation is the *same* as the speed of approach. Although the analysis above only considers the particular case when the velocities before and after collision are all in the same direction, you can see by imagining negative values for some of the velocities that it is true for all perfectly elastic collisions.

In a perfectly elastic collision, the speed with which the colliding objects separate is the *same* as the speed with which they initially approached each other.

> For a perfectly elastic collision
>
> Speed of separation = Speed of approach

This fact, together with the principle of conservation of momentum, can be used to predict the outcome of perfectly elastic collisions.

Example 2

Predict the outcome of this collision between trucks with spring buffers.

$\boxed{3m}\!\!\to u \quad \boxed{m}$

Solution

Assume the collision is perfectly elastic so the speed of separation must also be u.

$\boxed{3m}\!\!\to v \quad \boxed{m}\!\!\to v + u$

For conservation of momentum,

$$3mv + m(v + u) = 3mu$$
$$\Longrightarrow \qquad 3v + v + u = 3u$$
$$\Longrightarrow \qquad \qquad 4v = 2u$$
$$\Longrightarrow \qquad \qquad v = \tfrac{1}{2}u$$

giving speeds of $\tfrac{1}{2}u$ and $\tfrac{3}{2}u$, as shown.

$\boxed{3m}\!\!\to \tfrac{1}{2}u \quad \boxed{m}\!\!\to \tfrac{3}{2}u$

Exercise B (answers p. 90)

1   Consider the following three perfectly elastic collisions between trucks which each have spring buffers.

Before		After	

(a) $\boxed{m}\!\!\to u \quad \boxed{m}$ $\qquad\qquad$ $\boxed{m} \qquad \boxed{m}\!\!\to u$

(b) $\boxed{2m}\!\!\to u \quad \boxed{m}$ $\qquad\qquad$ $\boxed{2m}\!\!\to \tfrac{1}{3}u \quad \boxed{m}\!\!\to \tfrac{4}{3}u$

(c) $\boxed{m}\!\!\to u \quad \boxed{2m}$ $\qquad$ $\tfrac{1}{3}u \leftarrow\!\!\boxed{m}$ $\qquad$ $\boxed{2m}\!\!\to \tfrac{2}{3}u$

For each of the collisions above, show that

(i)   momentum is conserved

(ii) kinetic energy is conserved

(iii) speed of separation = speed of approach.

2 (a) Two trucks, each of mass m, approach each other from opposite
        directions, each travelling with speed v. Assuming the collision to
        be perfectly elastic, what will be the speed of each truck after the
        collision?

   (b) If the experiment is repeated with one of the trucks now having
        speed u, what will be the velocity of each truck after the collision?

   (c) Compare the total kinetic energy of the two trucks before and
        after each collision.

C Newton's law of restitution (answers p. 91)

If you drop a tennis ball, a lump of putty or a ball-bearing from the
same height on to a horizontal stone floor, they will all reach the
floor at the same speed. But we know from experience that the
speeds with which they rebound will be different for the different
materials.

Experiment shows that for a particular body striking a fixed surface at
right angles, the speed at which it rebounds is always the same fraction
of the speed before impact. This fraction (called the **coefficient of
restitution** and usually denoted by the letter e) is a constant for the
particular materials in collision. It is clear that $0 \leqslant e \leqslant 1$; for example,
putty dropped on stone has $e = 0$, while a 'Superball' on steel has
$e \approx 0.95$.

What happens when two moving bodies collide if they are moving in
the same straight line? It is found that the speed of separation is e times
the speed of approach.

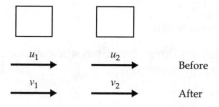

$$v_2 - v_1 = e(u_1 - u_2)$$

Example 3

A miniature railway truck, mass 2 kg, moving at 5 m s^{-1}, collides with
an engine, mass 8 kg, moving in the same direction at 0.5 m s^{-1}. After
the collision the truck rebounds at 1 m s^{-1}, Find the subsequent
velocity of the engine and the value of e for these two bodies.

Solution

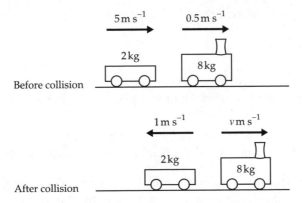

Before collision

After collision

The momentum equation is
$$2 \times 5 + 8 \times 0.5 = 2 \times (-1) + 8 \times v$$
giving $\qquad\qquad v = 2$

The speed of approach $= 5 - 0.5 = 4.5$ m s^{-1}; at these speeds, the truck and engine would have been 4.5 metres apart one second before impact. The speed of separation $= 2 - (-1) = 3$ m s^{-1}; one second after impact, they would be 3 metres apart.

So $e = \frac{3}{4.5} = \frac{2}{3}$

Example 4

4kg　　　　6kg

$4\,\text{m s}^{-1}$　　$1\,\text{m s}^{-1}$

Before

Two bodies collide as shown, Find their velocities after the collision if $e = \frac{1}{2}$.

Solution

It is not obvious in which direction the 4 kg body will move finally. We must make an assumption and form equations based on this.

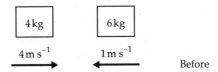

v_1　　　　v_2

Conservation of momentum: $\qquad 4v_1 + 6v_2 = 16 - 6 = 10$

Coefficient of restitution: $\qquad v_2 - v_1 = \frac{1}{2}(4 + 1) = 2\frac{1}{2}$

Solving, we get $v_1 = -\frac{1}{2}$, $v_2 = 2$.

The negative sign shows that the 4 kg body finally moves to the left, at a speed of $\frac{1}{2}$ m s^{-1}.

Exercise C (answers p. 91)

1   (a) A golf ball strikes a concrete floor at 5 m s^{-1} and rebounds at 3.5 m s^{-1}. Find e for the ball and the floor.

   (b) If this ball is dropped from a height of 2.5 m onto the same floor, find its speed on impact and the height to which it will then rise.

2   Drop a golf ball from eye level onto a stone or concrete floor and find how high it rises. Work out an approximate value for the coefficient of restitution. Repeat with a tennis ball or a 'Superball'.

3   A ball is thrown vertically downwards with a speed of 5 m s^{-1} from a height of 1 m and just rises to the same height when it bounces. Find the coefficient of restitution between the ball and the floor.

4   A miniature railway truck, mass m kg and speed 1 m s^{-1}, collides with another truck, mass 2 kg and speed 3 m s^{-1}, travelling in the opposite direction. If $e = \frac{1}{4}$ and the second truck is brought to rest by the collision, find the subsequent speed of the first truck. Find also its mass.

5   A ball of mass 2 kg, moving at 3 m s^{-1}, strikes a similar ball of mass 1 kg which is at rest. If $e = \frac{1}{2}$ and they both move off in the same direction, find the speed of each ball after the collision.

6   In each part of this question, you are given velocities before impact and the coefficient of restitution. Find the velocities after impact, the impulse on each body (equal to the change in momentum) and the kinetic energy lost.

	7 kg	3 kg	
(a)	3 m s^{-1} →	1 m s^{-1} →	$e = \frac{1}{2}$
(b)	2 m s^{-1} →	3 m s^{-1} ←	$e = 0.2$
(c)	2 m s^{-1} →	3 m s^{-1} ←	$e = 0.8$
(d)	3 m s^{-1} →	1 m s^{-1} →	$e = 0$
(e)	2 m s^{-1} →	3 m s^{-1} ←	$e = 0$
(f)	3 m s^{-1} →	7 m s^{-1} ←	$e = 1$

7 When $e = 0$, a collision is said to be **perfectly inelastic**. Then the speed of separation is zero, i.e. the bodies move off together. Find the fraction of the KE which is lost when a body hits another body of the same mass, which is initially at rest, if the impact is perfectly inelastic.

8 A ball is projected from level ground and hits a vertical wall at right angles.

Describe what happens if the impact is

(a) perfectly inelastic $(e = 0)$

(b) perfectly elastic $(e = 1)$

Where does the ball land if $e = \frac{2}{3}$?

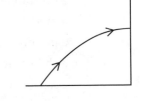

9E If a particle hits a fixed surface obliquely, the velocity component perpendicular to the surface is reversed and its magnitude is multiplied by e. The component parallel to the surface is unchanged.

A ball hits a wall at 10 m s^{-1}, at 70° to the surface. Find its speed and direction immediately after impact if $e = 0.6$.

10 A billiard ball hits two adjacent edges of a billiard table in succession. Show that if the coefficient of restitution in each case is e, then the final direction of travel of the billiard ball is parallel to its initial direction.

Discuss the assumptions you have made.

After working through this chapter you should

1 know that momentum is conserved in all collisions but kinetic energy is lost, except in a perfectly elastic collision

2 know that in a perfectly elastic collision, the speed of separation is equal to the speed of approach

3 know that for any pair of bodies colliding, the speed of separation is always the same fraction of the speed of approach, the fraction being called the coefficient of restitution of the bodies and denoted by e; in a perfectly elastic collision $e = 1$

4 know that an impact for which $e = 0$ is called a perfectly inelastic collision

5 when a ball bounces on a fixed surface, the speed immediately afterwards is e times the speed just before impact.

3 Circular motion

A Angular speed (answers p. 91)

Consider the following situations:

a car moving round a roundabout

a model aeroplane flying on a string

a person on a 'centrifuge' machine or a Big Wheel at a fair

a child swinging on a knotted rope hanging from a tree

a satellite orbiting the Earth.

All of these examples describe a situation which may be modelled as circular motion. In this chapter we investigate the motion of objects or particles moving in circles – most of them travelling with constant speed.

When any particle moves in a circle, it travels in a plane so that its distance from a fixed point, the centre, remains unchanged. Even if its speed is constant, the velocity vector is changing direction, as it is directed along the tangent to the circle. It is useful to define another quantity, called the angular speed, which measures the rate at which a line joining the particle to the centre is turning.

1 The revolution counter of a car shows an angular speed of 3000 revolutions per minute. Express this in radians per second.

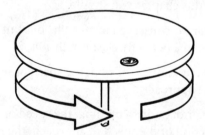

A penny is placed on the turntable so that its centre is 0.06 metre from the centre of the turntable. The turntable rotates through an angle of 2 radians every second.

2 What is the speed of the penny in metres per second?

3 What can you say about the velocity of the penny?

4 Where can you place a second penny so that
(a) its speed is half that of the first penny
(b) its speed is twice that of the first penny?

The motion of the penny can be plotted on a grid.

5 How long does it take the penny to reach $(0, 0.06)$?

6 Find the coordinates of the penny after
   (a) 0.5 second
   (b) 1 second
   (c) 2 seconds.

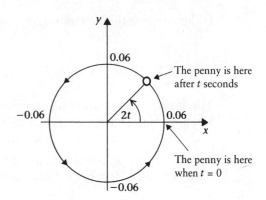

7 What are the coordinates of the penny after t seconds?

The position of the penny at any time t is defined by the vector **r**, measured in metres, where

$$\mathbf{r} = \begin{bmatrix} 0.06 \cos 2t \\ 0.06 \sin 2t \end{bmatrix}$$

The velocity $\mathbf{v} = \dfrac{\mathrm{d}\mathbf{r}}{\mathrm{d}t}$ and then **v** is measured in m s^{-1}.

$$\mathbf{r} = \begin{bmatrix} 0.06 \cos 2t \\ 0.06 \sin 2t \end{bmatrix} \Rightarrow \mathbf{v} = \begin{bmatrix} -0.12 \sin 2t \\ 0.12 \cos 2t \end{bmatrix}$$

8 Calculate the velocity vector **v** for time t where $t = 0.5, 1, 2$ seconds. Draw a circle to represent the penny on the turntable and show the positions from question 6 and the velocity vectors just calculated.

We use the Greek letter ω (omega) to represent angular speed. If a wheel rotates through angle θ in time t, then the average angular speed is ω, where

$$\omega = \frac{\theta}{t} \qquad \text{and} \qquad \theta = \omega t.$$

The instantaneous angular speed is the rate of change of angle,

$$\omega = \frac{\mathrm{d}\theta}{\mathrm{d}t}$$

When a particle moves around a circle of radius r, the displacement x around the circumference is given by

$$x = r\theta,$$

where θ is the angle turned through (see *Pure 1*, page 130).

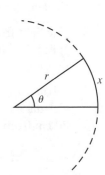

Differentiating this equation gives

$$\frac{dx}{dt} = r\frac{d\theta}{dt}$$

or $v = r\omega$.

This is the basic equation which connects linear and angular speeds, whenever any object moves in circular motion.

When a particle is moving round a circle of radius r and the angular speed is ω rad s^{-1}, the speed of the particle is given by

$$v = r\omega$$

One complete circuit of 2π radians will take $\dfrac{2\pi}{\omega}$ seconds.

Example 1

A wheel of radius 5 cm is rotating at 6 rpm. What is its angular speed in rad s^{-1} and what is the speed of the edge of the wheel?

Solution

6 rpm = $6 \times 2\pi$ or 37.7 radians per minute

i.e. $\dfrac{37.7}{60} = 0.628$ rad s^{-1} (to 3 s.f.)

The radius of the wheel is 5 cm, so in one second the edge of the wheel has moved a distance 5×0.628 cm. The speed is 3.14 cm s^{-1} (to 3 s.f.).

Exercise A (answers p. 92)

1   A helicopter's rotor blade is 4 metres long and is rotating at 50 rpm. Find the speed of the blade tip.

2   An outboard motor is started by pulling a cord wound around a grooved wheel of radius 10 cm. If the cord is pulled at 1 m s^{-1} what is the angular speed of the wheel in rad s^{-1}?

3   The light from a lighthouse appears to rotate around at a constant speed. It shines in my direction once every 5 s. Find its angular speed in rad s^{-1}.

4   A ballerina spins three and a half times about her own axis in 1.5 s. Calculate her average angular speed in rad s^{-1}. The tip of her toe is 70 cm from the axis of her spin. What is its linear speed?

5 A funfair roundabout is rotating with angular velocity 2.5 rad s^{-1}. How many revolutions will take place in a 30 s ride? Will is sitting in a car that is 4 m from the centre of the roundabout. What is his linear speed?

6 The drum of a washing machine can rotate at between 500 and 1000 rpm. What are these in rad s^{-1}? If the diameter of the drum is 1.2 metres, what is the range of speeds of points on the drum?

7 The Earth has radius 6.37×10^6 metres. It spins about its axis approximately once every 24 hours. What is the approximate speed of an object due to this rotation

(a) on the Earth's equator (b) at the north pole?

8E The cotton from a cotton reel of radius 2 cm is pulled out with a constant speed of 3 m s^{-1}. What is the angular speed of the reel in rad s^{-1}? If the radius of an empty reel is 1 cm and the reel takes 50 seconds to empty, sketch a rough graph of angular speed against time. Give reasons for your sketch.

B Acceleration (answers p. 92)

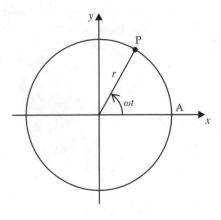

Consider a particle P moving about O in a circle radius r with uniform speed ω (starting from the x-axis).

The displacement $\mathbf{r} = \begin{bmatrix} r\cos\omega t \\ r\sin\omega t \end{bmatrix}$

1 Find the velocity by differentiation.

2 Show that the acceleration can be written as

$$\mathbf{a} = r\omega^2 \begin{bmatrix} -\cos\omega t \\ -\sin\omega t \end{bmatrix} \quad \text{or} \quad \mathbf{a} = -\omega^2 \mathbf{r}$$

What is its direction?

Show that its magnitude is $a = r\omega^2 = \dfrac{v^2}{r}$.

When a conker on the end of a string rotates in a circle at steady speed, the only force on it is the tension in the string. From $\mathbf{F} = m\mathbf{a}$, you should expect the acceleration to be in the direction of the string towards the centre. This is at right angles to the velocity, causing the conker to change direction without change of speed.

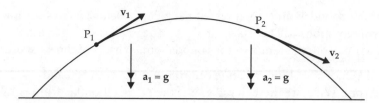

Compare this with projectile motion when the acceleration is **g**. At P_1, the acceleration has a component opposite to the velocity; this gives the rate at which the speed is decreasing. The component of acceleration perpendicular to the velocity determines how sharply the path is curving. At P_2 the path continues to bend but now the speed is increasing.

Acceleration in two dimensions always has this double significance. Motion in a circle with constant speed is a special case.

Example 2

A bicycle and rider of total mass 120 kg are rounding a bend of radius 20 m. The maximum sideways frictional force available is 600 N. Find the greatest linear speed of the bike before it will skid out of the bend.

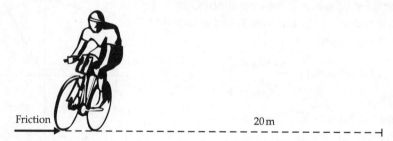

Solution

The problem is approached by setting up a model and using Newton's second law of motion. We assume the bicycle and rider can be modelled as a particle. By doing so, we cannot investigate the possibility of the bike toppling sideways; however, this is not asked in this question.

Suppose that the frictional force is exactly 600 N.

There is an acceleration $\dfrac{v^2}{r}$ towards the centre of the bend.

$$F = ma \text{ gives } 600 = 120 \times \frac{v^2}{20},$$

$$v = 10$$

So the maximum speed is 10 m s^{-1}.

Exercise B (answers p. 92)

1   In a device for simulating the accelerations produced in rocket flights, a horizontal arm of length 7 m is rotated about a vertical axis. If it is desired to produce an acceleration of 120 m s^{-2} (about 12 times the acceleration due to gravity), at what rate must the arm rotate?

2   What is the acceleration in m s^{-2} of an aircraft flying at a constant speed of 2000 km h^{-1} in a circular arc of radius 16 km?

3   A racing car is travelling at a constant speed of 120 km h^{-1} around a bend consisting of part of a circle. The magnitude of its acceleration is 30 m s^{-2}. What is the radius of the bend?

4   A roundabout in a children's playground is rotating at 10 revolutions a minute. The radius of the roundabout is 2 metres. A child of mass 30 kg sits on the seat. What are her speed and acceleration if she sits

(a) 1 metre from the centre

(b) 2 metres from the centre?

Describe how the force acting on the child alters as she changes her position on the roundabout.

5   A coin of mass 4 grams is placed on a turntable and rotates with constant angular speed 0.5 rad s^{-1}. Write down its acceleration in metres per second^2 when it is placed 15 cm from the axis of rotation. Calculate the magnitude of the resultant force on the coin. What can you deduce about the coefficient of friction between the turntable and the coin?

6   The coefficient of static friction between a block of wood and a turntable surface has been found to be 0.3 . The block is placed 20 cm from the axis of rotation and the speed of the turntable is gradually increased. How fast is it rotating when the block slides off?

7E A group of ten skaters have linked arms to form the rotating diameter of a circle.

(a) If they make one complete revolution every 6 seconds, describe the probable speeds of the various members of the group.

(b) What is the acceleration of the outside pair?

(c) Estimate the force needed to produce such an acceleration.

C Gravity (answers p. 93)

You know that, near the Earth's surface, a body falling freely will have an acceleration of about 9.8 m s^{-2} and that this is caused by the force of gravity. This force, the **weight**, acts whether the body is falling freely or not, and is equal to mg newtons if the mass of the body is m kg.

A body further from the Earth's surface, such as a spacecraft in orbit, experiences a smaller gravitational acceleration.

This section examines the force of gravity more generally.

Throughout history, astronomers have studied the motion of the planets. The Greeks assumed that the universe was geocentric, i.e. they assumed that the Earth was at the centre. In Alexandria, Claudius Ptolemy used this geocentric model to predict the motions of the planets, often with great accuracy. In fact the geocentric model remained dominant until 1543, when Copernicus claimed that the Sun, and not the Earth, was the centre about which the planets moved.

Later, in 1609, Johannes Kepler challenged the circular motion assumption. From observational data, Kepler realised that the paths of the planets were not perfect circles. He asserted that they move in elliptical orbits about the Sun.

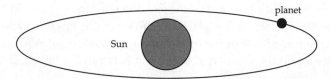

It became clear that the basic assumptions of the geocentric model were false. It was replaced by a heliocentric model in which the Sun is the centre of our solar system.

Newton developed a wider theory of gravitation which built upon the three laws of planetary motion of Kepler (1571–1630) and the observational data of Tycho Brahe (1546–1601) on the movement of planets.

Newton calculated that all of Brahe's data could be explained by assuming, as Copernicus first suggested, that the Sun was the centre of our planetary system, and that each planet is attracted to it by a force which is inversely proportional to the square of its distance from the Sun. He showed by mathematics that this same law explained the motion of the Moon around the Earth, Jupiter's moons around Jupiter, and the free flight of objects near to the Earth's surface – including apples falling from trees!

In 1667, Newton proposed a more general law of gravitation.

Newton's law of gravitation

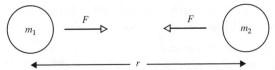

If two particles of mass m_1 kg and m_2 kg are at a distance r metres apart, they will attract each other with a force of magnitude

$$F = \frac{Gm_1 m_2}{r^2} \text{ newtons}$$

where G is a universal constant, called the constant of gravitation.

The value of the universal constant can be determined by a method introduced by Henry Cavendish in 1798. He set up an experiment where two small lead spheres each of mass 0.75 kg were hung from the ends of a 2 metre wooden rod. The centre of the rod was suspended by a long fine wire. When two heavy lead spheres, each of mass 250 kg, were placed near the two small spheres the attraction between the large and small spheres caused the rod to turn.

By measuring the twist in the wire he calculated the force of attraction and hence the constant G. He placed the experiment in a draught-free room and viewed the end of the rod from the garden, using a telescope.

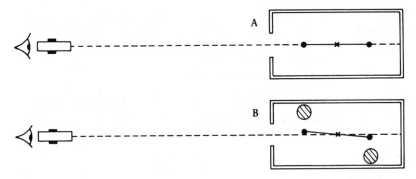

The work of Cavendish showed that G = 0.000 000 000 066 $N\,m^2\,kg^{-2}$, within 1% of its modern value of $6.673 \times 10^{-11}\,N\,m^2\,kg^{-2}$. This provided a direct verification of Newton's law of gravitation which had previously only been tested using astronomical data.

G, the universal gravitational constant in Newton's law of gravitation, has the value

$$G = 6.673 \times 10^{-11}\,N\,m^2\,kg^{-2}$$

The consequences of Newton's law are enormous. It says that *any* two bodies will attract each other, whether they are two planetary bodies like the Moon and the Earth, or two bodies on the Earth like the book and ball shown below.

The gravitational force on an object due to the Earth is called its weight.

The force of attraction between an object on the Earth's surface and the Earth itself is given by the equation

$$F = G\,\frac{mE}{R^2}$$

where m is the mass of the object, E is the mass of the Earth and R is the radius of the Earth.

The radius R was known to the ancient Greeks; it is approximately 6.4×10^6 metres. Since $F = mg$, it follows that

$$g = \frac{GE}{R^2}$$

As the Earth is not an exact sphere, R varies slightly, so g varies from 9.83 m s^{-2} at the North Pole to 9.78 m s^{-2} at the Equator. From now on, you should take $g = 9.8$ m s^{-2} (unless otherwise instructed) and understand that the consequent limit of accuracy is 2 significant figures.

1   Use Cavendish's value for G to determine the mass of the Earth.

2   Calculate the force of attraction between the Moon and an astronaut of mass 80 kg standing on its surface, using the following data.

> Mass of Moon $= 7.34 \times 10^{22}$ kg
> Approximate radius of Moon $= 1738$ km

How does this compare with the force of attraction due to the Earth that he would experience while standing on the Earth's surface?

Example 3

A rocket orbits the Earth at twice the radius of the Earth. At what speed is it travelling? (Assume the Earth is a sphere of radius $R = 6400$ km.)

Solution

$$r = 2R \quad \Longrightarrow \quad r^2 = 4R^2$$

So the weight of the rocket is one quarter of its value on Earth. Since the orbit is a circle, the acceleration is $\dfrac{v^2}{r}$.

$$F = ma \text{ gives } \frac{mg}{4} = \frac{mv^2}{r}$$

$$v^2 = \tfrac{1}{48}gr = \tfrac{1}{4} \times 9.8 \times 12.8 \times 10^6$$

$$v = 5600 \text{ m s}^{-1}$$

Exercise C (answers p. 93)

Take $G = 6.67 \times 10^{-11} \text{ N m}^2 \text{ kg}^{-2}$, $g = 9.80 \text{ m s}^{-2}$ and the Earth as a sphere of radius 6380 km.

1   (a) A 4 kg mass is allowed to fall from rest. What is its change in momentum after 3 seconds?

   (b) During the same time interval, the Earth experiences an equal but opposite change in momentum. Assuming that the Earth has a mass of 5.98×10^{24} kg, what is the effect on the Earth's velocity?

2   The weight of a 1 kg stone is 9.80 N at sea level.

   (a) Calculate its weight
      (i)   at the top of the Eiffel Tower (322 m above sea level)
      (ii)   at the top of Mount Everest (8.848 km above sea level)
      (iii) at the edge of the stratosphere (928 km above sea level).

   (b) Calculate its weight in a space capsule orbiting the Earth in a circular orbit whose radius is twice the radius of the Earth.

   (c) Sketch a graph of weight against distance above sea level for a 1 kg mass, using the values given above.

3   The Moon's mass is approximately $\frac{1}{80}$ that of the Earth, and its radius is about $\frac{3}{11}$ that of the Earth. If a man of 60 kg were to stand on the surface of the Moon, estimate what his weight would be relative to the Moon.

4   A rocket of mass 400 kg is travelling in a circular orbit around the Earth at an altitude of 1000 km above the Earth's surface. Find the mutual force of attraction between the Earth and the rocket, and the linear speed of the rocket.

5   A spaceship orbiting at 4000 km above the Earth's surface uses a booster rocket to change orbit to one at 3500 km above the Earth's surface. If the new orbit is stable, explain why the rocket's speed has increased, and find the percentage change of speed.

6   (a) Calculate the angular speed of the Moon about the Earth. (One revolution takes 27.3 days.)

   (b) Use the result $a = r\omega^2$ to calculate the acceleration of the Moon. (The radius of the Moon's orbit $= 3.84 \times 10^8$ metres.)

   (c) Calculate a value for the mass of the Earth.

7   Take 1 year as 365 days, and the average distance between the centres of the Sun and the Earth as 1.50×10^8 km. Calculate a value for the mass of the Sun.

8   A satellite circles the Earth with angular speed ω rad s^{-1} at a distance r metres from the centre of the Earth.

Show that $r^3 \omega^2 = GE = gR^2$, where E is the mass of the Earth and R is its radius.

9   A 'stationary' communications satellite circles the Earth above the equator with a period of one day, so that it is always directly above the same point. Find its height and speed.

10 Kepler's third law states that $\dfrac{T^2}{D^3}$ is constant, where T is the time for a complete revolution of a planet about the Sun and D is its mean distance from the Sun.

Show that this is true if it is assumed that the planets move in circular orbits.

After working through this chapter you should

1   know that for a particle rotating in a circle of radius r with constant angular speed ω,

$$\text{speed} = v = r\omega,$$

$$\text{acceleration} = \frac{v^2}{r} = r\omega^2,$$

$$\text{time for one revolution} = \frac{2\pi}{\omega}$$

2   know that, for circular motion as above, linear velocity is directed along the tangent and the linear acceleration is towards the centre of the circle

3   be able to apply Newton's laws of motion to various situations involving circular motion

4   know that Newton's law of gravitation states that

$$F = \frac{Gm_1 m_2}{r^2}$$

where G is a universal constant called the constant of gravitation.

4 Centres of mass

A Moments (answers p. 94)

Up to now, you have modelled various objects, in motion and at rest, by considering them to be **particles**. There are situations when this model must be extended.

If you watch from the side as one person throws a tennis racket through the air to another person, does it behave like a projectile?

If it did, you would expect to see a parabolic path. Here, however, the rotation of the racket itself makes it difficult to see exactly what happens.

If you tried this in practice it would be helpful to have a marker, for example a red dot, on the racket and to watch it move through the motion. However, where would you place the red dot?

If you placed it on the lower part of the handle then its path would look something like this.

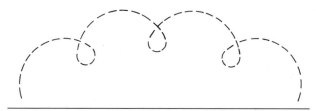

Alternatively, you could place the marker at the 'balance point' for the racket – the point about which the weight of the racket is equally distributed. In this case, the path of the dot *would* appear to be a simple parabola.

The balance point is called the **centre of gravity**. The gravitational forces on the different parts of an extended body behave like a single force, the weight, acting at the centre of gravity.

One of the important properties of a particle is that it does not have shape or size. This means that you can think of all the forces as acting at a single point. However, it also means that you cannot take into account any rotational motion which might be caused by the forces.

A **rigid body** is an extended body which has a fixed size and shape. Where forces act on a body to try to rotate it, you may have to take into account the size and shape of the body in question and model it as a rigid body.

The particle model used previously is not always suitable for rigid bodies. If a body is modelled as a particle, the forces acting on it are concurrent, whereas for an extended body you will find that the points of application of the forces are as important as their magnitudes. This section considers a different model; one which can be applied to rigid bodies in both static and dynamic situations. This model is referred to as the **rigid body model**.

Consider a heavy rod on a smooth table with two forces of magnitude P acting as shown in the plane of the table.

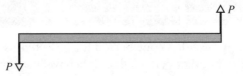

The sum of the forces is zero, but the rod will start to turn and so is not in equilibrium. The two forces have a turning effect on the rod.

If the effect of a force being applied to an object is to cause it to rotate about a pivot, then this effect is called the **moment of the force about the pivot**. A pivot is a line or axis through a particular point.

The moment of a force about an axis, O, is the product of the magnitude of the force applied and the perpendicular distance between the line of action of the force and the axis, O.

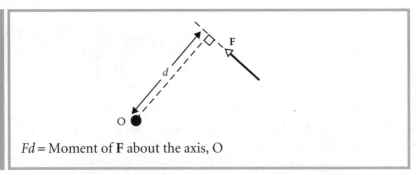

Fd = Moment of **F** about the axis, O

The sense of a moment is either clockwise or anticlockwise. By convention anticlockwise is taken as positive.

The units of a moment are newton metres (N m).

When a particle is not moving, the total of all the forces on it, added vectorially, is zero. This applies also to a rigid body. However, if there is a resultant moment about any axis, then the body will rotate.

If it does not rotate, the clockwise moments must exactly balance the anticlockwise moments.

Example 1

A drawbridge of mass 500 kg and length 5 m is to be winched into the upright position by two cables. The cables make an angle of 35° with the bridge and are attached to the bridge 4 m from the pivot, P. What is the moment of the weight of the drawbridge about the hinge? What is the tension in each cable when the drawbridge is just off the support on the right?

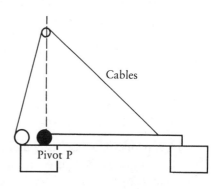

Solution

Assume that the bridge is uniform and that the cables are light. There are four forces acting on the bridge when it is on the point of being raised; its weight, the tensions in the two cables, and a reaction, $\mathbf{R}$, at the hinge. Assume that $g = 9.8$ m s^{-2}.

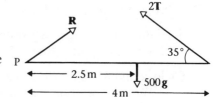

Moment of the weight about the pivot, P = 500 $g \times 2.5$
$$= 12\ 250 \text{ N m clockwise}$$

Anticlockwise moment about P $= 2T \times 4 \sin 35°$.

So $2T \times 4 \sin 35° = 12\ 250$
$$T = 2670 \text{ N}$$

Note that, since $\mathbf{R}$ acts through the pivot P, it has no turning effect about P.

Exercise A (answers p. 94)

1   Bob and Sally are pushing open an enormous gate hinged at A with forces as shown in the diagram.

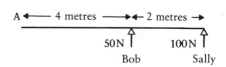

Calculate the total turning effect of the forces on the gate about the pivot at A.

2   A uniform rod OA is pivoted at O and held at an angle ϕ to the vertical (as shown) by a horizontal force P newtons.

If OA $= 2a$ metres, find the moment of the weight $\mathbf{W}$ and the force $\mathbf{P}$ about the axis through O. (The force at O has been omitted from the diagram.)

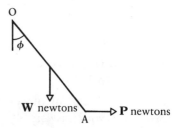

3   Find the moment of each force shown in the
    diagram about

    (a) the pivot point O

    (b) the point A.

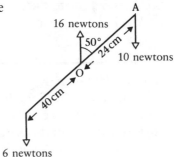

4   A plank of length *l* is lying horizontally on the
    ground and is pivoted at one end. Bronwen lifts
    up the other end with a force **T** newtons at an
    angle ϕ as shown.

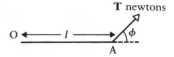

    Find the moment of **T** about the pivot O. At what angle should she
    apply the force in order to maximise the turning effect?

5   Carole lifts a wheelbarrow full of brick rubble (combined mass 90 kg).
    Estimate the lifting force.

6   Josie and her son Winston are on a
    swing see-saw. Josie has mass 60 kg and
    Winston 20 kg. Does the gravitational
    force acting on Winston or that acting
    on his mother provide the greater
    moment about the pivot when the
    see-saw is in the position shown?

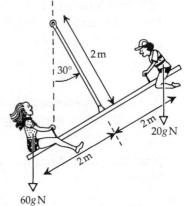

7

    Josie (in the question above) makes a
    simple see-saw by placing a 3 m plank
    of wood on a pivot which is positioned
    closer to her than to her son.

    (a) How close to Josie should the pivot be placed if the see-saw is to
         balance?

    (b) The plank of wood is quite heavy. Does this make a difference to
         your answer?

B Centre of gravity (answers p. 95)

'Josie is 2 m from the pivot.'

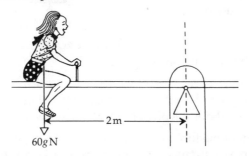

2 m

60g N

A statement like this really means that Josie's **centre of gravity** is 2 m from the pivot. The gravitational pull on the woman acts on all parts of her, but, from the point of view of taking moments about a pivot, the effect of the gravitational pull is that of a single force acting at the centre of gravity.

The position of the centre of gravity of the human body is important. Many of the movements you make throughout the day are purely to make small adjustments to the position of your centre of gravity in order to maintain balance.

You can alter the position of your centre of gravity by changing your shape, but the centre of gravity of a rigid body is a fixed point, no matter what the orientation of the body or how it is moving.

The following example illustrates how you can calculate the location of the centre of gravity of a compound object.

Example 2

An object consists of a 400-gram mass on one end of a rod and a 100-gram mass on the other. The rod itself is a uniform cylinder of mass 100 g and length 40 cm. The locations of the centres of gravity of the individual masses and of the rod are shown on the diagram below, but where is the centre of gravity when the three of them together form 'a single object'? Take $g = 10 \text{ m s}^{-2}$.

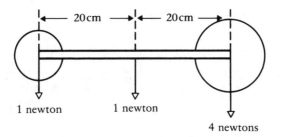

20 cm 20 cm

1 newton 1 newton

4 newtons

Solution

Suppose the object is pivoted about the
left-hand end of the rod.

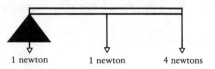

1 newton   1 newton   4 newtons

The moment of the weight on the left will be zero because its line of
action passes through the pivot.

The moment of the largest weight will be $4 \times 0.4 = 1.6$ N m clockwise.
The moment of the rod itself will be $1 \times 0.2 = 0.2$ N m clockwise. Thus
the total moment about the pivot is 1.8 N m clockwise.

The total gravitational force acting on the object is 6 newtons, so if the
centre of gravity is a distance d metres from the pivot, it follows that
the moment of the object as a whole about the pivot is $6 \times d$. This
must be the same as the sum of the moments of the parts of the object
about the pivot, so

$$6 \times d = 1.8 \quad \Rightarrow \quad d = 0.3$$

The weighted rod will behave as though a single force of 6 newtons
was acting at a point 30 cm along its length measured from the centre
of the 100-gram mass. It is this point, the centre of gravity, which will
obey Newton's laws of motion and follow a parabolic path if the rod is
thrown.

1   For the weighted rod of Example 2, take the pivot at any point you
    choose and check that you obtain the same position for the centre of
    gravity.

> The centre of gravity of a compound body is the point at which
> the total weight of the body can be said to act. If the body is
> symmetrical, it lies on the line, or lines, of symmetry of the body.
>
> The moment of the weight of the whole body about *any* pivot, O,
> is equal to the sum of the moments of the weights of the
> component parts of the body about O.

Exercise B (answers p. 95)

1   Find the centre of gravity of the following objects.

(a)   (b)

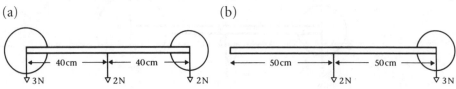

2 (a) A light ruler has weights placed on it as shown. It is pivoted at the left-hand end and is supported in equilibrium by a force A at the other end. Find A.

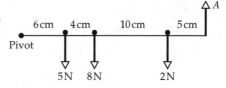

(b) It is now pivoted at the right end and supported at the left end. Find the force B.

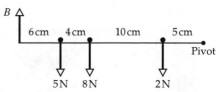

(c) This time it rests on supports at each end. What are the forces C and D?

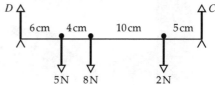

3

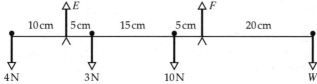

A light ruler rest on two supports and carries weights as shown.

(a) Find E and F when $W = 5$ N.

(b) Find E and F when $W = 10$ N.

(c) W is gradually increased until the ruler rotates. When does this happen?

4 The diagram shows a person standing upright with both arms stretched out sideways parallel with the ground.

Axes are drawn with the person facing in the direction of the x-axis, and with the origin vertically below the person's centre of gravity.

The arms are moved as indicated. All movements are from this original starting position.

(a) Both arms are rotated through 90° to a vertically upward position.

(b) The right arm is lowered to a vertically downward position.

(c) The left arm is held horizontally outwards towards the front.

(d) The left arm is lowered to a vertically downward position and the right arm is held horizontally outwards towards the front.

For each of the movements, describe whether the displacement of the centre of gravity from its *original* position is positive, negative or zero in the direction of the x-, and y- and z-axes.

C Centre of mass (answers p. 95)

A space platform orbiting the Earth consists of three spherical modules attached to a rigid connecting walkway as shown in the diagram. (The walkway is of negligible mass compared with the mass of the modules.) Suppose that the gravitational force per unit mass is g newtons.

In the absence of further information you can assume that

(a) the masses of the three modules are m_1, m_2 and m_3

(b) the distances of the centres of gravity of the modules are x_1, x_2 and x_3 from the end of the walkway.

You can find the centre of gravity of the space platform by taking moments about the imaginary pivot O shown in the diagram.

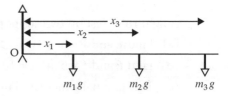

Total moment $= m_1 g x_1 + m_2 g x_2 + m_3 g x_3$ clockwise.

If the centre of gravity is located a distance $\bar{x}$ from O then

$$(m_1 g + m_2 g + m_3 g)\bar{x} = m_1 g x_1 + m_2 g x_2 + m_3 g x_3$$

$$\bar{x} = \frac{m_1 x_1 + m_2 x_2 + m_3 x_3}{m_1 + m_2 + m_3} = \frac{\Sigma\, mx}{\Sigma\, m}$$

Note that $\bar{x}$ is independent of g, and so the gravitational attraction makes no difference to the position of the centre of gravity.

The position where

$$\bar{x} = \frac{\Sigma\, mx}{\Sigma\, m}$$

is also referred to as the centre of mass of the object.

The assumption made in solving the problem is that g is constant in magnitude and direction. This is reasonable when the object is near a much larger body such as the Earth or the Moon.

However, if the space platform was in deep space near an asteroid of comparable size then the gravitational force per unit mass would not be constant for the whole of the platform and the orientation of the body would affect the position of the centre of gravity.

Note that the position of the centre of mass of a body is always the same but that of the centre of gravity can vary in exceptional circumstances.

The notation $\bar{x}$ used above for the x-value of the centre of mass is the same as that used for the mean in statistics.

1 The number of customer complaints, x, received per day by a firm was recorded for 200 working days. The frequencies, f, were as in the table.

x	f
4	18
5	38
6	61
7	46
8	23
9	14
	200

(a) Calculate the mean number of complaints, m.

(b) Draw the histogram on cardboard and mark on it the line $x = m$.

(c) Cut out the histogram and show that it balances on the edge of a ruler placed along the line $x = m$.

The masses of the rectangles in the histogram are proportional to the frequencies, so the formula for the mean

$$\bar{x} = \frac{\Sigma\, fx}{\Sigma f}$$

gives the same result as the formula for the centre of mass

$$\bar{x} = \frac{\Sigma\, mx}{\Sigma m}.$$

Example 3

Find the centre of mass of a uniform lamina (thin sheet) in the following shape.

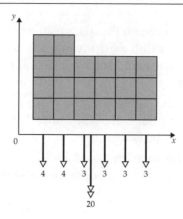

Solution

x	m	mx
1	4	4
2	4	8
3	3	9
4	3	12
5	3	15
6	3	18
	20	66

$$\bar{x} = \frac{\Sigma\, mx}{\Sigma\, m} = \frac{66}{20} = 3.3$$

The six weights shown above are equivalent to a single weight of 20 in the position shown.

Now turn the lamina over.

y	m	my
1	6	6
2	6	12
3	6	18
4	2	8
	20	44

$$\bar{y} = \frac{44}{20} = 2.2$$

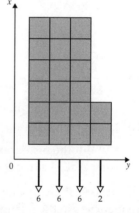

2   In what sense is the point G $(\bar{x}, \bar{y})$ the mean of the lamina?

If a body can be modelled as a number of rigidly connected point masses m_1, m_2, m_3, m_4 ... located at points $(x_1, y_1), (x_2, y_2)$ ... then the centre of mass will be located at $(\bar{x}, \bar{y})$ where

$$\bar{x} = \frac{\Sigma\, mx}{\Sigma\, m} \qquad \bar{y} = \frac{\Sigma\, my}{\Sigma\, m}$$

Under normal circumstances the position of the centre of gravity is independent of the gravitational force per unit mass and hence is the same as the position of the centre of mass, and can be calculated in the same way. The two terms are used interchangeably.

The centre of mass of the lamina in Example 3 can be found in many ways. The origin can be taken elsewhere and the shape can be divided up differently.

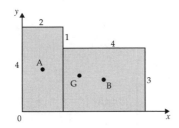

Mass 8 at A $(1, 2)$
Mass 12 at B $(4, 1\frac{1}{2})$

$$\bar{x} = \frac{8 \times 1 + 12 \times 4}{8 + 12} = 2.8$$

$$\bar{y} = \frac{8 \times 2 + 12 \times 1\frac{1}{2}}{8 + 12} = 1.7$$

3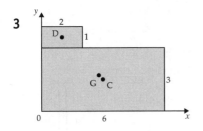

Calculate $\bar{x}$ and $\bar{y}$ based on this diagram for the same lamina.

4 Draw the lamina of Example 3 on graph paper. Mark on it the points A, B, C, D, G. Show that G lies on AB and on CD.

Exercise C (answers p. 95)

1 Find the centre of mass of each of the following laminae.

(a)

(b)

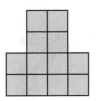

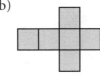

(c)

(d)

(e)

(f)

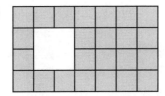

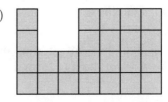

2 A balancing toy is made by soldering two uniform spheres to an L-shaped wire as shown. A small metal pin of negligible mass is to be soldered to the longer arm so that its point is at the centre of gravity of the object.

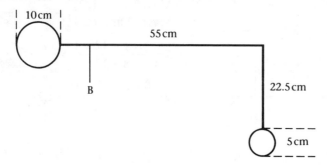

If the mass of the wire can be ignored and the spheres have masses 20 grams and 80 grams, find the length and position of the balance pin, B.

3 A pendulum consists of a disc of mass 0.2 kg and radius 5 cm attached to a uniform rod of mass 0.1 kg and length 0.9 m. The centre of the disc is at one end of the rod. Find the centre of mass of the pendulum.

4 A hammer has a mass of 0.8 kg (head and handle combined). Distances are as shown. The centre of mass of the hammer is 30 cm from the end of the handle. Find the mass of the handle.

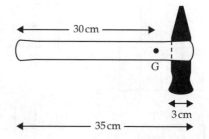

5 A thin uniform wire of length 120 cm is bent to make a triangle with sides 30 cm, 40 cm and 50 cm. Find how far the centre of mass is from the nearest vertex.

6 (a) Find the centre of mass of a lamina in the shape of this T.

   (b) Find the centre of mass of a wire of length 16 units bent to form the outline of the T.

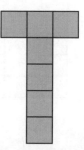

7E 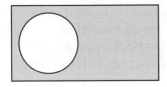 A circle of radius 4 cm is cut out of a rectangular lamina 20 cm by 10 cm. The centre of the circle is 5 cm from three of the sides. Find the centre of mass of the lamina. You may take the area of the circle to be 50 cm^2.

D Applications (answers p. 96)

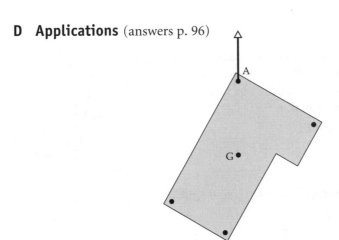

1   Draw the figure of Example 3 on cardboard and mark the centre of mass G on it. Cut it out and make small holes near the corners.

Suspend the lamina by a thread through one hole. What do you notice about G?

Repeat, suspending the lamina from each corner in turn.

2   Conduct an experiment to find the approximate position of the centre of mass of an upright chair by balancing it first on its front legs and then on its back legs.

The gravitational forces on the various parts of the lamina above are equivalent to a single force acting through G. In equilibrium, this force must have zero moment about A, so G must be vertically below A.

A box is placed on a rough table, and one end of the table is gradually raised. When will the box topple?

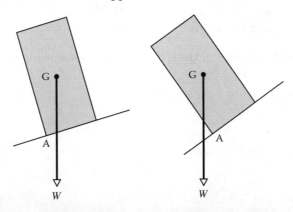

When the vertical line through the centre of mass is to the right of the lowest edge of the box, as in the first diagram, the moment of the weight about A is clockwise and the box does not tip. Tipping would take place in the situation shown in the second diagram. In both cases, of course, we are assuming that the surfaces are rough enough to prevent slipping.

Example 4

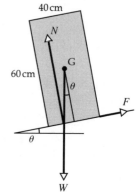

A uniform box has a square base of side 40 cm and height 60 cm. It is at rest on a rough slope inclined at an angle θ. The lowest edge of the box is horizontal. The coefficient of friction, μ, is 0.7.

What can you say about θ?

Solution

Since the box does not tip, $\tan \theta \leqslant \frac{20}{30}$; so $\theta \leqslant 33.7°$.

$F = W \sin \theta$ and $N = W \cos \theta$

Since the box does not slip, $\dfrac{F}{N} \leqslant \mu$; so $\tan \theta \leqslant 0.7$, $\theta \leqslant 35.0°$

It follows that $\theta \leqslant 33.7°$. If the table is tilted more and more, the box will tip before it slips.

Exercise D (answers p. 96)

1   Cut a triangle out of cardboard and find its centre of mass experimentally. What do you notice about this point?

2

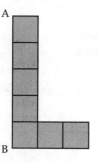

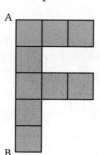

(a) A lamina in the shape of the L shown above is suspended from A. Find the angle that AB makes with the vertical.

(b) Repeat for the letter F shown above.

3 Two removal men are carrying a loaded rectangular box at a steady rate up a flight of stairs, inclined at 45° to the horizontal. The loaded box is of weight 750 newtons, its length is 2 m and its square ends have edges of length 0.8 m.

Calculate the part of the weight supported by each of the hands of each man if they are holding the underneath of each square end. What assumptions are you making?

What do the results suggest about the position for the stronger man of the two?

4 (a) A car weighing 6800 N has its axles 3 m apart. If its centre of gravity is 1.2 m in front of the rear axle, what force will be exerted by the road on each wheel? What assumptions are you making?

   (b) If luggage of weight 600 N is placed on the roof rack so that its weight acts through the centre of gravity of the car, what force will then be exerted on each wheel by the road?

   (c) If the luggage is placed centrally in the boot so that its weight acts at a distance of 0.6 m beyond the rear axle, what force will then be exerted on each wheel by the road?

5 A man's forearm is 0.3 m from the elbow joint to the palm, its weight is 27 N and its centre of gravity is 0.13 m from the joint. The biceps muscle, which raises the forearm, is 0.02 m from the joint. Assume that the forearm is horizontal and the biceps muscle is vertical.

Find the tension in the biceps

   (a) when the hand is empty

   (b) when a weight of 45 N is held in the palm.

6

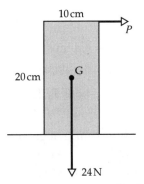

An empty box of weight 24 N is on a rough table. The coefficient of friction is $\frac{1}{3}$.

A horizontal force P is applied to the middle of a top edge. The box neither slips nor tips. What can you say about the magnitude of P?

7

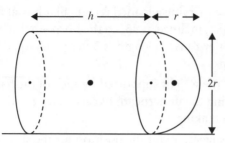

The diagram shows an open container consisting of a thin cylindrical shell of radius r and height h joined to a hemispherical shell of radius r made from the same metal and of the same thickness.

The centre of mass of the hemispherical shell is $\frac{1}{2}r$ from its base.

Find the centre of mass of the container and what will happen if it is placed on a horizontal table with its axis horizontal, given

(a) $h = 2r$

(b) $h = \frac{1}{2}r$

(c) $h = r$.

After working through this chapter you should

1 know that the moment of a force about a pivot is the product of the magnitude of the force and the distance between the pivot and the line of action of the force (units are usually in newton metres, i.e. N m)

2 be able to find the total moment of several forces about a pivot by summing the individual moments (it is conventional for anticlockwise moments to be taken as positive and clockwise moments as negative)

3 know that, for an object to be in equilibrium,
- the sum of the forces acting upon it must be zero
- the sum of moments of these forces about any pivot must be zero

4 know that the centre of gravity of a body is the point at which the total gravitational force on the body appears to act

5 be able to find the position of the centre of gravity of an object by using moments and understand that the centre of mass and centre of gravity of an object are normally coincident where

$$(\bar{x}, \bar{y}) = \left(\frac{\sum mx}{\sum m}, \frac{\sum my}{\sum m} \right)$$

5 Variable forces in one dimension

A Impulse (answers p. 97)

For a constant force **F** acting on a body for time t, the change in momentum is equal to the product **F**t. This is called the **impulse** of the force. The units of momentum have so far been given as kg m s^{-1} (from mv). It is more usual to use the equivalent N s (from **F**t) as the units for both impulse and momentum.

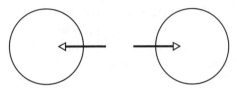

When two bodies collide, the force on one is equal and opposite to the force on the other (Newton's third law). The forces act for the same time interval, so the impulses are equal and opposite. That is why the total momentum is unchanged.

It is important to remember that impulse and momentum are vector quantities.

1D A ball of mass 0.1 kg hits a wall at right angles at 9 m s^{-1}. It rebounds at 5 m s^{-1}. Find the impulse and the average force on the ball if it is in contact with the wall for 0.01 s.

2

A 5 kg body travelling at 5 m s^{-1} hits a stationary 3 kg body as shown. If its speed is reduced to 2 m s^{-1}, find the impulse on the first body and the average force if the period of contact is 0.006 s.

State the impulse on the second body and its speed after the impact.

3 A ball of mass 0.5 kg is moving with velocity $\begin{bmatrix} 8 \\ 4 \end{bmatrix}$ m s^{-1} when it receives a blow that changes its velocity to $\begin{bmatrix} 4 \\ 6 \end{bmatrix}$ m s^{-1}.

What is the impulse due to the blow?

4 A hockey ball of mass 0.15 kg is moving horizontally at 10 m s^{-1} when it is hit. Immediately afterwards, the ball is moving horizontally at 15 m s^{-1} in the direction shown.

Find the impulse on the ball and the average force if the time of contact is 0.005 s.

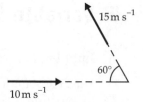

For the rest of this chapter we will consider one-dimensional motion, so momentum and force only vary in magnitude.

When a tennis ball hits a wall, it is deformed and then springs back to its original shape. The force between the ball and the wall increases from zero to a maximum then decreases back to zero. The same happens less noticeably when a hockey stick hits a ball. How should impulse be defined when a force varies?

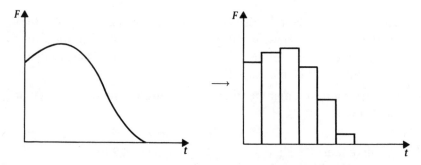

The variable force shown in the graph can be approximated by a series of forces, constant over short time intervals. The area of each rectangle of the step graph represents an impulse and so the total change in momentum is given by the total area under the (time, force) graph.

Thus the impulse is $\int F \, dt$.

Example 1

Measurements taken during a simulation of a car crash produced the graph shown opposite.

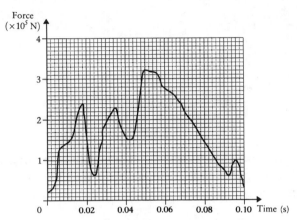

The mass of the car was 1200 kg. Estimate the original speed of the car if it came to rest after 0.1 second.

Solution

The area under the graph can be estimated by counting squares or using trapezia.

The area under the graph is approximately 17 000 N s.

So $17\,000 \approx 1200v$, where v is the original speed.

$$v \approx 14 \text{ m s}^{-1}$$

For one-dimensional motion, the impulse $\int F\,dt$ is represented by the area under a (time, force) graph. It is equal to the change in momentum.

Example 2

The force acting on a golf ball of mass 45 g when it is struck may be modelled approximately by the function

$$F = 10^{11}\, t(t - 0.004)^2 \qquad 0 < t < 0.004$$

Find the velocity with which it leaves the club.

Solution

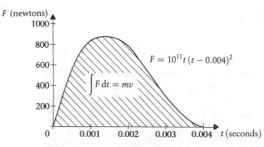

The area under the graph gives the change in momentum, or impulse. Since the initial velocity (and hence momentum) is zero, the momentum of the ball when it leaves the club face is represented by the area

$$mv = 10^{11} \int_0^{0.004} t(t - 0.004)^2 \, dt$$

$$0.045v = 2.13 \qquad \text{(see question 5, below)}$$

$$\Rightarrow \qquad v = 47 \text{ m s}^{-1}$$

The ball leaves the club face with an initial velocity of 47 m s^{-1} in the direction of the force.

5   By multiplying out and integrating, show that $\int_0^a t(t - a)^2 \, dt = \frac{1}{12}a^4$,

   if a is a constant. Verify that this equals 2.13×10^{-11} when $a = 0.004$.

Exercise A (answers p. 98)

1   A cricket ball of mass 0.15 kg is moving horizontally at 30 m s^{-1} when the batsman hits it. Find the impulse if the ball is

   (a) stopped dead

   (b) hit straight back towards the bowler at 20 m s^{-1}.

2   A ball of mass 90 grams strikes a wall at right angles when moving at 8 m s^{-1}. It rebounds along the same line with a speed of 6 m s^{-1}. A very simple force–time model assumes that the force between the wall and the ball increases uniformly with time up to a maximum and then decreases at the same rate. Use this model to estimate the maximum force (in newtons) on the ball if the total contact time is 0.002 second.

3   A car of mass 1 tonne started from rest and accelerated for 60 seconds. During this time the propulsive force was measured at 10-second intervals.

Force (N)	1050	650	480	260	170	130	80
Time (s)	0	10	20	30	40	50	60

Use this information to estimate the final speed of the car.

4   Find the total impulses provided by the forces in each of the graphs.

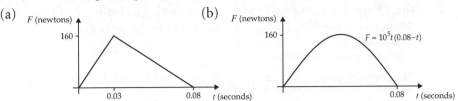

5   When an archer releases the bow-string, the force on the arrow is initially 200 newtons. The string is in contact with the arrow for 0.1 second. Three models are suggested for the force–time equation during this period.

(a) $F = \dfrac{40}{t + 0.1} - 200$

(b) $F = 200 - 200 \sin 5\pi t$

(c) $F = 250e^{-kt} - 50$ where $k = 10 \ln 5$

In each case show that $F = 200$ when $t = 0$,
                       and $F = 0$ when $t = 0.1$.

Find the impulse suggested by each model and the speed imparted to an arrow of mass 0.3 kg.

6   An impulse of magnitude 4 N s is applied to a ball of mass 0.15 kg moving at 20 m s^{-1}. Find the final velocity of the ball if the impulse is at right angles to the initial velocity.

B   Work done by a variable force (answers p. 98)

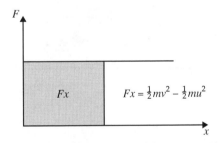

For a constant force **F**, acting in the direction of the displacement x, the area under the (displacement, force) graph is the work done and equals the change in kinetic energy. Considering a (displacement, force) graph will help you to see how to calculate the work done by a variable force.

A car of mass 1 tonne, starting from rest, experiences a net forward force **F** (taking account of resistances to motion). During the first 50 metres of motion, the force is as given in the table below.

Distance travelled (metres), x	5	15	25	35	45
Net forward force (newtons), F	3800	3675	3500	3275	3000

1 Estimate the speed of the car after it has travelled 10, 20, 30, 40 and 50 metres.

2 How would you expect the result
$$Fx = \tfrac{1}{2}mv^2 - \tfrac{1}{2}mu^2$$
to generalise for a variable force?

You saw earlier that the area under a (time, force) graph represents the change in momentum.

$$\int F\,dt = mv - mu$$

For a constant force, this simplifies to
$$Ft = mv - mu$$

Similarly, for a force *in the direction of displacement,* the area under a (displacement, force) graph represents **work done** and equals the change in **kinetic energy** (which is a scalar quantity).

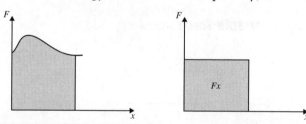

$$\int F\,dx = \tfrac{1}{2}mv^2 - \tfrac{1}{2}mu^2$$

For a constant force, this simplifies to
$$Fx = \tfrac{1}{2}mv^2 - \tfrac{1}{2}mu^2$$

The change in momentum and the change in kinetic energy equations can both be shown to be integrals of Newton's second law of motion, $F = ma$.

$$F = ma = m\frac{dv}{dt}$$

$$\Rightarrow \quad \int F\,dt = \Big[mv\Big]_u^v = mv - mu$$

Also, $F = m\dfrac{dv}{dt} = m\dfrac{dv}{dx}\dfrac{dx}{dt}$

$$= mv\dfrac{dv}{dx} \text{ since } v = \dfrac{dx}{dt}$$

So $\displaystyle\int F\,dx = \int mv\dfrac{dv}{dx}\,dx = \int mv\,dv$

$$= \left[\tfrac{1}{2}mv^2\right]_u^v$$

$$= \tfrac{1}{2}mv^2 - \tfrac{1}{2}mu^2$$

Example 3

A car of mass 1 tonne, starting from rest, experiences a resultant force F newtons. During the first 50 metres of motion, the force is related to the distance travelled, x, by the relationship $F = 4025 - x^2$.

Calculate the speed of the car after it has travelled 50 metres.

Solution

Total work done $= \displaystyle\int_0^{50} (4025 - x^2)\,dx$

$$= \left[4025x - \tfrac{1}{3}x^3\right]_0^{50} \approx 159\,600\text{ J}$$

Total work done = change in kinetic energy

$$159\,600 = \tfrac{1}{2} \times 1000 \times v^2 - 0 \implies 319.2 = v^2$$

The speed is approximately 17.9 m s^{-1}.

Exercise B (answers p. 99)

1 An object of mass 10 kg is accelerated from rest by a machine with the following force–distance relationship.

Distance (metres)	0	1	2	3	4	5	6	7	8
Force (newtons)	400	300	240	210	190	160	130	80	0

Estimate the speed of the object at intervals of one metre during the thrust.

2 A particle moves along the x-axis and when it is x m from O it is acted on by a force F N. Find the work done when the particle goes from $x = a$ to $x = b$ given

(a) $F = 5x$, $a = 0$, $b = 6$ (b) $F = 30 - 3x$, $a = 0$, $b = 2$

(c) $F = \dfrac{120}{x^2}$, $a = 2$, $b = 8$ (d) $F = -9x$, $a = 5$, $b = 1$

3   The effective force forward, F newtons, on a van of mass 1.4 tonnes accelerating from rest, is given by the equation $F = 4000 - 22.5x - 0.25x^2$, where x metres is the distance travelled from rest.

Find, by integration, the speed achieved by the van when it has gone 50 metres.

4   A car of mass 1 tonne starts from rest on a level road. The net forward force initially is 3300 newtons but this falls linearly with the distance travelled so that after 200 metres its value is zero. Find the force in terms of x. Hence find the speed of the car every 50 metres and sketch a graph to show the relationship between the speed and the distance travelled.

5   The propulsive force F N on a bullet reduces as it moves along the barrel. A simple model is given by $F = 4000 - kx$ where k is a constant and x m is the distance moved.

Given that the bullet has mass 0.015 kg and that it leaves the barrel (which is 0.6 m long) at 500 m s^{-1}, find the value of k.

In questions 6–9, take the weight of a mass m kg at a distance x m from the centre of the Earth as $\dfrac{mgR^2}{x^2}$ N, where $g = 9.8$ m s^{-2} and the radius of the Earth, $R = 6.4 \times 10^6$ m.

6   Find the work done on a satellite of mass 1000 kg when it is lifted up to 200 km above the Earth's surface.

7   A projectile is fired vertically upwards at an initial speed of 3000 km h^{-1}. Neglecting atmospheric resistance, find how high the projectile rises.

8   A moon probe is launched by a rocket. Find the speed that the probe must have when the rocket motors cut out if it is to escape from the Earth's gravitational field. Discuss your assumptions.

9   A meteorite of mass 30 kg falls directly towards the centre of the Earth.
   (a) Find the work done by gravity while it falls from 1000 km above the Earth's surface.
   (b) Find the speed with which the meteorite would hit the Earth if air resistance was negligible. Assume that the initial speed is small.
   (c) Meteorites do not in fact hit the Earth at great speed. What happens to the energy?

C Springs and elastic strings (answers p. 100)

You know that when a string or spring is being
stretched, there is a force called **tension**. This exerts
equal and opposite forces at the ends.

Similarly, when rods and springs are compressed,
there is an outward force called a **thrust**.

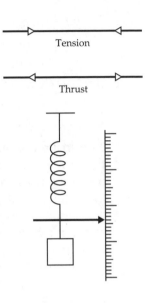

1 Conduct experiments with various springs and
   elastic strings to see how much they stretch when
   different weights are suspended.

2 Are the scales of spring balances and butchers' scales
   linear? Explain.

Experiments show that, when a spring is stretched,
the tension is approximately proportional to the
extension; under compression, the thrust is
proportional to the amount by which the spring is
compressed. The constant of proportion is the same
in both cases.

Robert Hooke (1635–1703) is credited with the discovery of these
relations, summarised by the formula

  $T = kx.$

Here T is the tension and x the extension (negative values of T and x
represent thrusts and compressions), and k is a constant depending
only on the material and geometric properties of the spring.

> The tension or thrust in a spring is proportional to the extension
> of the spring.
>
> $T = kx$
>
> where k is called the spring constant.

This relation does not apply if the tension or thrust is excessive. Any
spring or elastic string will have an 'elastic limit' beyond which
Hooke's law breaks down.

Example 4

The top end of a spring is fixed and the lower end is extended
by 3 cm and attached to a mass of 10 kg. Given that the
spring is extended by 2 cm under a tension of 80 N, what will
be the acceleration of the mass immediately it is released?

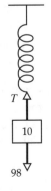

Solution

The force (in newtons) exerted by the spring $= 80 \times \frac{3}{2} = 120$.

The forces acting on the mass are

$\qquad$ 120 N upward and 98 N downward.

If the acceleration is a m s^{-2} upwards, the equation of motion is

$\qquad 120 - 98 = 10a$.

Hence $a = 2.2$; the acceleration is therefore 2.2 m s^{-2} upwards.

Note that this is only the initial acceleration. As the spring contracts, the tension and consequently the acceleration are reduced. Soon the position is reached where the acceleration is zero; by this time the mass has acquired an appreciable velocity and continues to rise. But then the tension will be less than the weight, there will be a deceleration ... and so on. In fact the mass will oscillate. In practice there will be internal forces in the spring (called damping forces) which oppose this oscillation and cause it to die away. What will be the final extension?

Exercise C (answers p. 100)

1   A spring is extended by 2 cm when under a tension of 40 N. By how much will it be extended under tensions of 60 N, 80 N, 10 N?

2   A spring has constant 80 N m^{-1} and unstretched length 30 cm. Find its length when

(a) stretched by a force of 8 N

(b) compressed by a force of 2 N.

What force will stretch it to a length of 38 cm?

3   A spring of unstretched length 20 cm, has length 22 cm when held vertically and supporting a mass of 5 kg at its lower end. What will its length be when supporting 3 kg? Express the spring constant in N m^{-1}.

4   An elastic rope is 2 m in length when unstretched and extends by 1 cm when under a tension of 150 N.

(a) What will its length be when held vertically and made to support a mass of 5 kg at the lower end?

(b) What will the acceleration of the mass be immediately after release, if it is pulled down until the rope is extended by 2 cm and then released?

5   A spring that requires a thrust of 100 N to compress it by 3 cm, is compressed by 4 cm and locked in that position. It is placed vertically on a table and a mass of 8 kg is fixed to the top end. What will the initial acceleration of the mass be when the spring is released?

D **Elastic potential energy** (answers p. 100)

If you stretch a bow, the (positive) work done by the pull you apply (in the direction of displacement) will be equal and opposite to the (negative) work done by the tension in the bow. However, the tension, like gravity, does not disappear once motion stops; it has the *potential* to do positive work. Such energy is called **elastic potential energy** (abbreviated to EPE) and this is the energy which is transferred to the arrow as kinetic energy when the bow is released.

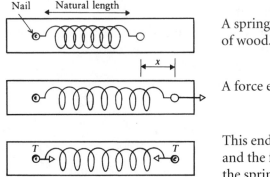

A spring is anchored by a nail to a strip of wood.

A force extends the spring a distance x.

This end is also anchored with a nail, and the force is removed. The tension in the spring is $T = kx$.

In this situation there is a store of potential energy. The tension in the spring has the potential to do some work if, for example, one end is connected to an object which is free to move when the nail is removed.

If this were to happen, then the tension would decrease linearly from kx to zero as the displacement of the object increased from zero to x.

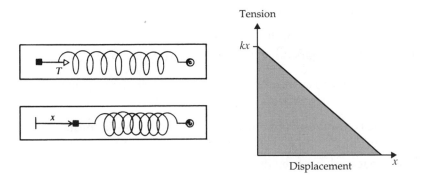

Work done by tension = Area under the graph

$$= \frac{kx^2}{2}$$

The tension in the spring has the potential to do $\dfrac{kx^2}{2}$ joules of work.

> The work done to extend a spring by a distance x is
> $$\tfrac{1}{2}kx^2$$
> This is the elastic potential energy (EPE) of the extended spring.

Example 5

A spring of length 10 cm is stretched to a length of 12 cm by a pull of 10 newtons.

(a) What is its spring constant?

(b) What work must be done to stretch it a further 2 cm?

Solution

(a)
$$T = kx$$
$$\text{So } 10 = k \times 0.02$$
$$\Rightarrow \quad k = \frac{10}{0.02} = 500 \text{ N m}^{-1}$$

(b) Work done to stretch the spring to 12 cm $= 500 \times \dfrac{(0.02)^2}{2} = 0.1$ J

Work done to stretch the spring to 14 cm $= 500 \times \dfrac{(0.04)^2}{2} = 0.4$ J

Work done to stretch the spring from 12 cm to 14 cm $= 0.3$ J

Exercise D (answers p. 100)

1 A spring has a spring constant of 100 N m^{-1}.
   (a) What is the work done if it is stretched by 5 cm?
   (b) What is the work done if the spring is stretched by 15 cm?

2 The work done to stretch an elastic band by 10 cm from its natural length is 0.2 joules. What is its spring constant?

3 A spring is compressed by a distance of 5 cm. Its spring constant is 500 N m^{-1}.
   (a) What work has been done?
   (b) What work must be done to compress it by a further 5 cm?

4 A catapult consists of a light elastic string of length 20 cm fixed to the ends A and B of prongs 16 cm apart. The elastic constant is 600 N m^{-1}.
   A small stone of mass 40 grams is placed at the mid-point M of the string and pulled back as shown.

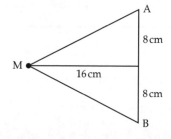

(a) Find the length of the string and the elastic potential energy in this position. Find also the tension in the string.

(b) The stone is released. If the kinetic energy of the stone on leaving the catapult is equal to the EPE in (a), find the speed of the stone at this moment.

5E Find the initial acceleration of the stone in question 4 when it is released.

6 A spring has unstretched length 15 cm and spring constant 250 N m^{-1}.

A body of mass $\frac{1}{2}$ kg is suspended from one end of the spring, the other end being fixed. The body is held with the spring vertical and neither stretched nor compressed; it is then suddenly released.

(a) When the body has dropped 2 cm, it is moving with speed $v \text{ m s}^{-1}$.

Explain why KE gained = PE lost − EPE gained .

Hence find v .

(b) Find the speed when the body has fallen 3 cm.

(c) Find the greatest extension of the spring.

After working through this chapter you should

1   know that for one-dimensional motion, the area under a (time, force) graph represents the change in momentum, or impulse,

$$\int F\,dt = mv - mu$$

2   know that for one-dimensional motion, the area under a (displacement, force) graph represents work done and equals the change in kinetic energy,

$$\int F\,dx = \tfrac{1}{2}mv^2 - \tfrac{1}{2}mu^2$$

3   know that a spring with spring constant k newtons per metre has a tension kx newtons when it is stretched by an amount x metres. When it is compressed x metres, it has a thrust of kx newtons.

In either case, its elastic potential energy (EPE) is $\tfrac{1}{2}kx^2$ joules.

6 Modelling circular motion

A Motion in a horizontal circle (answers p. 100)

This chapter is concerned with combinations of forces associated with circular motion. Remember that a body moving with constant speed v round a circle of radius r has an acceleration towards the centre of $\frac{v^2}{r}$; this can also be expressed as $r\omega^2$ where ω is the angular speed.

1   A penny of mass 3.5 grams is placed on a turntable 0.12 m from the axis of rotation. The speed of the turntable is gradually increased until the penny starts to slide. The angular speed is then 4 rad s^{-1}.

(a) What are the forces acting on the penny? Calculate the acceleration of the penny just before it starts to slide.

(b) Find the coefficient of friction.

(c) If the penny is moved to a point 0.2 m from the axis, at what angular speed will it now start to slide?

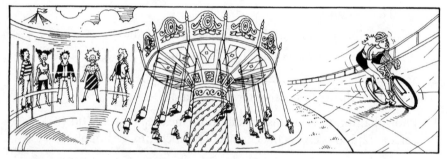

Understanding circular motion can be of practical benefit. For example, how can you design a chair-o-plane (pictured in the centre above) which is safe, or a cycle track with the correct angle of banking to ensure that the cycles actually stay on the track? In these situations, circular motion can be fun, but is it safe? To answer this question it is necessary to analyse the forces involved.

A designer of a chair-o-plane at a fun-fair might ask questions such as

● Will a child swing out at a greater angle than a much heavier adult?
● Will the people on the inside swing out at the same angle as those on the outside?
● Will empty chairs be a problem?
● What will happen as the speed increases?

Some insight into the first question can be gleaned from analysing the motion of a conical pendulum.

If you tie a small mass or bob to the end of a piece of string and set the bob moving in a horizontal circle, then you have a conical pendulum.

Two forces act on the bob: its weight and the tension in the
string. Your hand feels an 'outward' and 'downward' force due
to the tension in the string pulling your hand. This is equal and
opposite to the 'inward' and 'upward' force you apply to the
string to pull the bob around in a circle. This is an example of
Newton's third law of motion. If the angular speed of the bob
is increased, then the radius of the circular motion also
increases. You could also keep the angular speed the same but
change the length of the string.

Example 1

A conker of mass 10 g is attached to one end of a
string of length 50 cm. The other end is held fixed,
while the conker makes horizontal revolutions below,
with the string at 30° to the vertical. Find the tension
in the string, and the angular velocity of the conker.

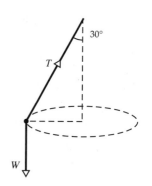

Solution

The radius of the circle is 50 sin 30° cm = 0.25 m.

The acceleration is horizontal, so the vertical
component of T exactly balances the weight W.

$$T \cos 30° = W = 0.01g, \text{ giving } T = 0.113 \text{ N}.$$

The tension has a horizontal component $T \sin 30°$ and this is linked to
the acceleration by Newton's second law

$$T \sin 30° = 0.01 \times 0.25\omega^2.$$

This gives $\omega = 4.8$, an angular speed of 4.8 rad s^{-1}.

2 (a) Repeat Example 1, taking the mass as m kg, the length of the
string as l m and the angle as θ. Show that $\omega^2 = \dfrac{g}{l \cos \theta}$

  (b) Calculate θ given that $l = 0.4$, $\omega = 6$.

  (c) What happens to the angle θ as the angular speed ω increases?

  (d) How big can the angle become?

  (e) What happens if you keep the angular speed the
same but increase the length of the string?

3 (a) Does a heavy bob swing out at the same angle as a
light bob if they are both rotating at the same
angular speed and the strings are the same length?

  (b) If the lengths are different, is it possible for the
lighter bob to move in a lower circle than the
heavier bob?

Sometimes, a mathematical analysis of a problem suggests 'solutions' to new problems. For example, it is interesting to note that for the conical pendulum,

$$\cos \theta \leqslant 1 \Rightarrow \omega \geqslant \sqrt{\frac{g}{l}}$$

4 What happens if $\omega < \sqrt{\frac{g}{l}}$?

What does this tell you about the motion of a conical pendulum?

5 What is the main difference between a chair-o-plane and a conical pendulum?

Exercise A (answers p. 101)

1 A car travelling at 15 m s^{-1} is going round a bend, which is part of a circle of radius 150 m. Find the sideways frictional force on the tyres given that the car has mass 1000 kg.

2 A fairground machine consists of a large hollow cylinder of internal radius 5 metres. This can be made to rotate about its axis and a floor can be raised or lowered. When stationary, a door opens to allow a man of mass 75 kg to enter and then closes flush with the wall. The cylinder rotates faster and faster until the friction between the man's back and the wall is equal to his weight. Then the floor drops away.

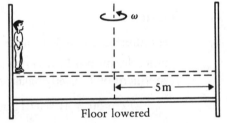

Floor lowered

Draw a force diagram showing the weight, normal reaction and friction force acting on the man. Given that the coefficient of friction is $\frac{2}{5}$, find the angular speed when the floor can first drop.

3 A conical pendulum has length 80 cm and a bob of mass 0.5 kg, which is rotating in a horizontal circle of radius 30 cm. Find the angle between the string and the vertical, the tension in the string and the linear speed of the bob.

4 A thin string of length 1 metre has a breaking strain of 60 newtons. A mass of 4 kg is attached to one end and made to rotate as a conical pendulum. Find the largest angular speed that can be attained and the angle the string makes with the vertical in this case.

5 A cyclist is rounding a bend of radius 10 metres. The road is banked at an angle of 30°. The total mass of the cyclist and the bicycle is 100 kg. The speed of the cyclist is such that there is no frictional force acting sideways on the cycle tyres up or down the slope.

The force diagram is given; it is just like the one for a conical pendulum. Find the normal contact force and the speed of the cyclist.

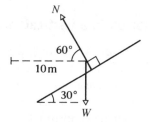

6 Find the angle of banking of a bend of radius 30 m if a cyclist travelling at 12 m s^{-1} experiences no sideways frictional force up or down the slope on his bicycle.

7 Part of a large slide at a swimming pool consists of a horizontal semicircle of radius 4 m. The slide at this point is banked at 45°. Find the linear speed that a girl of mass 60 kg would have round the bend, given that she experiences no sideways friction. Does the girl's mass affect the answer?

8 A smooth hemispherical bowl is fixed with its rim horizontal. An object of mass 90 g slides in horizontal circles on the inside of the bowl at 140 rev min^{-1}. If the internal radius of the bowl is 20 cm, find the depth of these circles below the rim.

9 A simple pendulum is hung from the roof of a car. When the car rounds a bend at 54 km h^{-1}, the pendulum makes an angle of 20° to the vertical. Find the radius of the bend.

10E If a track curves in a horizontal circle of radius 300 m, at what angle should it be banked so that there may be no tendency to side-slip at a speed of 40 m s^{-1}? If in fact it is banked at 20°, what sideways frictional force will be necessary for a car of mass 1400 kg moving at 40 m s^{-1}?

11 A satellite moves in a circular orbit of radius 7000 km around the Earth. Taking the Earth's radius to be 6400 km, and assuming that the acceleration due to gravity varies inversely as the square of the distance from the centre of the Earth, calculate the velocity of the satellite in m s^{-1}. How long does it take to complete one orbit?

12 An ice-puck of mass 0.15 kg is attached by a light string of length 2 m to a point O on an ice rink. It is rotating in a circle with centre O with the string horizontal. The string has elastic constant 200 N m^{-1}.

(a) Find the angular speed of the puck if the string is stretched to a length of 2.1 m.

(b) Find the stretched length of string when the angular speed is 10 rad s^{-1}.

13E A conical pendulum has a bob of mass 0.2 kg on an elastic string. The string has unstretched length 0.5 m and elastic constant 40 N m^{-1}.

Find the length of the string and the angle made with the vertical when the angular speed is 6 rad s^{-1}.

B Motion in a vertical circle (answers p. 102)

In Section A you looked at some examples of bodies in horizontal circular motion – the chair-o-plane, conical pendulum, rotor, cyclist on a circular track – and in each case the speed was assumed to be constant. By contrast, when bodies move in a vertical circle their speed may change continually.

When tackling the more complicated problems in circular motion, an important principle to use is the conservation of mechanical energy. This is illustrated in the following example.

A small smooth marble of mass 6 grams is released from A, just below the rim of a hemispherical bowl, the axis of which is vertical. The inner radius of the bowl is 30 cm.

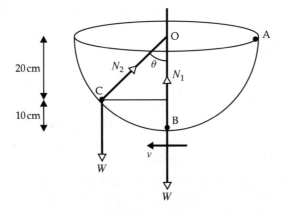

1D Use an energy equation to find the speed of the marble at its lowest point B. Is the normal reaction then greater than, less than or equal to the weight?

At B, the speed is at a maximum so the rate of change of speed is zero. Consequently, the acceleration is $\dfrac{v^2}{r}$ towards the centre and Newton's law gives

$$N_1 - W = \frac{mv^2}{r}$$

2 Check that at B the normal reaction is three times the weight of the marble.

Now let us find the speed and normal reaction at C, 10 cm above B. Assume that friction is negligible.

For the motion from A to C,

$$\text{KE gained} = \text{PE lost}$$
$$\tfrac{1}{2}mv^2 = mg \times 0.2$$
$$v^2 = 0.4g$$

The only forces are the weight and normal reaction. When the marble is rising, it is obviously slowing down. The deceleration is linked to the component of W in the tangential direction by Newton's law.

It can be shown that when a particle moves along a circular path it has an acceleration component $\dfrac{v^2}{r}$ towards the centre. This is true whether or not the speed is changing. So here, Newton's law in the radial direction gives

$$N_2 - W \cos \theta = \frac{mv^2}{r}$$

$$N_2 = mg \times \frac{20}{30} + \frac{m \times 0.4g}{0.3}$$

$$= 2mg$$

$$= 0.12 \text{ newtons}$$

For a particle moving in a circle of radius r with instantaneous angular speed ω,

$$\text{speed} = v = r\omega,$$

$$\text{acceleration component towards the centre} = \frac{v^2}{r} = r\omega^2$$

The tangential component of acceleration equals the rate of change of speed, $\dfrac{dv}{dt}$.

Exercise B (answers p. 102)

1 A Big Wheel at a fair rotates in a vertical plane at a rate of 1 rad s^{-1}. A man of mass 75 kg sits in a chair which is 5 m from the axle of the wheel. Find the horizontal and vertical reaction forces acting on the man at the top, bottom, half-way up and half-way down.

2 A boy swings on the end of a 5 m rope in a gymnasium. If he initially jumped off a 'horse' 2 m high at 3 m s^{-1} on a level 3.5 m below the point of suspension of the rope, which was taut, find

(a) his maximum speed

(b) his maximum height above ground

(c) the tension in the rope in the vertical position if his mass is 60 kg.

3   A girl swings a conker around in a vertical circle. The conker has mass 10 grams and its velocity is 3 m s^{-1} downwards when the string is horizontal. The string is 50 cm long and the conker hits another when it makes an angle of 120° with the upward vertical. Find

(a) the conker's velocity at this point

(b) the tension in the string at this point.

4   A bridge over a river is in the form of a circular arc of radius 20 m. A motor cycle and rider have total mass 200 kg. Calculate the normal reaction on the cycle (treated as a particle) when it is at the highest point of the bridge when its speed is (a) 5 m s^{-1} (b) 10 m s^{-1}.

What is the greatest speed at which it can cross the bridge without leaving the road at the highest point?

5   A demolition gang operates a crane with a 1 tonne bob on the end of a cable. The centre of mass of the bob is 10 m from the end of the jib and the mass of the cable can be neglected. Assuming that the bob travels along the arc of a vertical circle, with centre at the stationary extremity of the jib, starting 3 m above the lowest point, find an expression for v^2, the square of the speed of the bob, after it has descended 1 m, 2 m, and 3 m. At each of these points find the tension in the cable.

Will the cable snap if it has a breaking strain of 20 000 N and the bob is released to swing from a height of 5 m above the lowest point of the arc?

6   A rope of length 6 m is suspended from a high branch of a tree and a boy swings on the rope along the arc of a vertical circle starting from a branch 2 m above the lowest point of swing. When the rope is vertical it strikes against a branch situated 2 m below the point of suspension. If the boy releases his grip when the lower part of the rope makes an angle of 45° with the vertical, find the boy's speed at this instant.

7   A marble is placed on the top of a smooth up-turned hemispherical bowl and gently pushed off. If the radius of the outside of the bowl is 20 cm and the marble is of mass 2 g, find the speed v and normal reaction N after descending through a vertical distance of 4 cm.

If at time t, θ is the acute angle between the radius to the marble and the vertical, find v and N in terms of θ. Find the value of θ when the marble leaves the bowl.

8   If the marble of question 7 is given an initial speed of 1 m s^{-1} at the top, find where it leaves the bowl.

9   An olympic athlete of mass 70 kg is swinging in vertical circles on the high horizontal bar. Assuming that his motion can be described as the same as a mass of 70 kg concentrated at a distance of 120 cm from the bar, find the tension or thrust in his arms at the top and bottom of the circle given that the angular speed of the athlete at the top is

(a) 0.5 rad s^{-1} (b) 1 rad s^{-1}.

What must be the angular speed at the top if the athlete's arms are to remain just in tension throughout the motion? What would be the tension in his arms at the lowest point of swing in this case?

10 A bob of mass m is attached to one end A of an inextensible string of length l, the other end of which is attached to a fixed point O. The bob is projected horizontally with a velocity u when OA is vertical with A below O. Show that the velocity v of the particle when AO makes an angle of θ with the downward vertical through O is given by the expression

$$v^2 = u^2 - 2gl(1 - \cos\theta)$$

provided that the string is still taut. Apply Newton's second law radially at this point to show that the tension T in the string in terms of m, g, θ, u and l is given by

$$T = mg(3\cos\theta - 2) + \frac{mu^2}{l}.$$

(a) What can you say about u if the bob never rises above O? Describe the motion in this case.

(b) What can you say about u if the bob makes complete revolutions?

(c) Draw a diagram to show the position of the bob when the string goes slack given that $u^2 = 3gl$. Find an expression for the speed at this instant. Show on your diagram what happens next.

After working through this chapter you should

1 know how to set up and analyse a mathematical model for horizontal circular motion (e.g. a conical pendulum) where more than one force is acting on a body travelling with constant speed

2 know that if gravity is the only force doing work on a particle travelling in a vertical circle, then the speed at any point can be found by using the principle of conservation of mechanical energy

3 know that when an object moves in a circular path, its acceleration has two components: a radial component of magnitude $r\omega^2$ towards the centre of the circle and a tangential component of magnitude $\dfrac{dv}{dt}$

4 be able to apply Newton's second law to problems involving motion in a vertical circle.

7 Energy transfer

A Elastic potential energy (answers p. 103)

In the last chapter, you used conservation of mechanical energy in the context of motion in a vertical circle. Earlier, you saw that a spring or elastic string with elastic constant k has elastic potential energy $\frac{1}{2}kx^2$ when it is stretched an amount x.

Elastic potential energy (EPE) is now used in energy equations.

1D A catapult has a light elastic string of length 20 cm and elastic constant 600 N m^{-1}. The string is stretched to a total length of 35 cm and released, propelling a stone of mass 50 grams.

(a) Find the EPE in the stretched string.

(b) Find the speed with which the stone leaves the catapult.

(c) If the stone is shot straight up, find the greatest height reached by equating the PE gained with the EPE lost.

(d) If the stone is shot at an angle so that the maximum height reached is 6 m, find its speed at its highest point.

Elastic potential energy is entirely converted into kinetic energy in part (b) above, into gravitational potential energy in part (c) and into a combination of the two in part (d).

Energy appears in many different forms. Heat and electrical energy are both forms of energy. Some substances possess energy which can be released when they undergo a chemical change; for example, when coal is burnt it releases energy in the form of heat and light. A person has a similar store of 'chemical energy' which can be released in the form of mechanical energy when movement is required.

Energy is continually changing from one form to another. When you push a pencil across the table the chemical energy you release is changed into heat energy. (The temperatures of both the table and the pencil increase due to the action of friction.) When you lift a pencil up, the chemical energy released is changed into gravitational potential energy. This can be changed into kinetic energy if the pencil is allowed to fall. Gravitational potential energy and kinetic energy are both forms of **mechanical energy**. A spring has mechanical energy when extended or compressed.

Many problems are very much easier to solve if you can assume that mechanical energy is conserved. While this may be a reasonable assumption in many situations, you need to check carefully that energy is not added to the system from outside and that there are no dissipative forces (such as friction) which would change the energy from mechanical energy to a different form of energy such as heat or light.

If there are no dissipative forces, such as friction, and no energy is added from outside, then the total mechanical energy of a system is conserved.

Example 1

A marble travels down a chute from A to B.

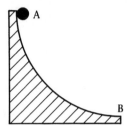

What assumptions are made if it is assumed that the decrease in PE is equal to the increase in KE?

Solution

You would assume that

(i)   the chute is smooth, so there is no friction

(ii) there is no air resistance.

There would, in practice, be some doubt about the validity of these assumptions. Although air resistance *is* likely to be negligible, the assumption of a smooth chute is unlikely to be valid and so any analysis based on this assumption must be interpreted accordingly.

The presence of friction will mean that not all of the decrease in potential energy will be converted into an increase in kinetic energy. Some of it will be 'lost' to other forms of energy. If the marble slides, mechanical energy will be lost to heat energy; if the marble rolls it will gain 'rotational' kinetic energy as well as 'translational' kinetic energy. Either way, the speed of the marble at the bottom of the chute will be less than expected.

Example 2

A 200 gram mass is attached to the end of a spring (natural length 0.3 metre) and hangs at rest (in equilibrium). The mass is then pulled down a distance 0.15 metre (to position A) and released. The mass oscillates as shown. Assume the spring obeys Hooke's law, with spring constant 8 N m^{-1}.

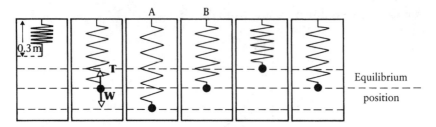

What is the resultant force acting on the mass when it is in position B and what is its velocity at that time?

Solution

Position B is the equilibrium position, so the resultant force is zero (i.e. the tension in the spring is equal and opposite to the gravitational pull).

For simplicity we will take $g = 10$ m s^{-2} in this example. Then

$$0.2g = 8x \implies x = 0.25.$$

The spring is extended 0.25 m beyond its natural length when the mass is in position B.

Being in equilibrium does not mean the mass is not moving. The direction of its motion is obvious. The problem is how to calculate the magnitude of the velocity.

As no energy from outside is put into the system once it is in motion and as energy loss due to air resistance is negligible, it is reasonable to assume that the total mechanical energy of the system is constant.

(In fact, mechanical energy is gradually lost, mostly as heat. In the short term, however, this is a reasonably good model.)

Position A

KE $\quad \dfrac{mv^2}{2} = 0$

PE $\quad mgh = 0 \quad$ (relative to position A)

EPE $\quad \dfrac{kx^2}{2} = \dfrac{8 \times 0.4^2}{2}$

$\qquad\qquad = 0.64$ joules

Position B

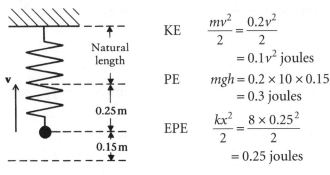

KE $\dfrac{mv^2}{2} = \dfrac{0.2v^2}{2}$
$= 0.1v^2$ joules

PE $mgh = 0.2 \times 10 \times 0.15$
$= 0.3$ joules

EPE $\dfrac{kx^2}{2} = \dfrac{8 \times 0.25^2}{2}$
$= 0.25$ joules

Total mechanical energy at A = total mechanical energy at B
$$0.64 = 0.1v^2 + 0.3 + 0.25$$
$\Rightarrow$ $\qquad\qquad 0.9 = v^2$

The velocity of the mass is 0.95 m s^{-1}.

Exercise A (answers p. 103)

1

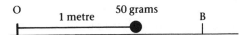

The diagram shows a mass of 50 grams lying on a smooth table. It is fixed to point O by an elastic string of length 1 metre. It is held at point B by a force of 4 newtons and then released. OB is 1.5 metres.

At what speed is the mass travelling when it passes O?

2 A child's toy rocket (mass 20 grams) is fired by releasing a compressed spring. The natural length of the spring is 5 cm, the compressed length is 1 cm and the spring constant is 1000 N m^{-1}.

Estimate the height the rocket will reach when fired vertically up in the air.

3 A light spring, of natural length 0.2 m, is extended to a length of 0.3 m when a mass of 100 g is hung on it. It is then pulled down a further 0.1 m and released.

(a) Find the velocity of the mass when the spring next has length 0.3 m.

(b) Where is its elastic potential energy greatest?

4 A mass of 2 kg is hung from a spring with spring constant 500 N m^{-1}.

(a) Find the extension when the mass hangs in equilibrium.

(b) The mass is pulled down until the extension is 0.1 m and then released. Find the speed of the mass when the spring reaches its unstretched length.

5 A stunt actor attaches one end of a nylon rope to himself and the other end to an anchor point on the edge of the roof of a high-rise building. He then steps off the roof and falls vertically. The actor has mass 78 kg and the roof is 200 metres above an air bag on the ground. The rope has

unstretched length 100 metres and its tension, T newtons, when stretched by a further x metres, is given by the formula

$$T = 30x$$

(a) Given that the actor reaches the air bag, calculate the loss of PE of the actor and the gain in EPE of the rope.

(b) Hence estimate the speed with which the actor hits the air bag.

6   A spring has natural length 0.5 m and spring constant 400 N m^{-1}. One end is attached to a fixed support and the other to a mass of 10 kg. The mass is released when it is 0.5 m below the support. Calculate the speed of the mass when it has fallen 0.2 m and find where it comes instantaneously to rest.

7   An elastic string hangs vertically, supporting a bob of mass 0.6 kg. The unstretched length is 30 cm and in equilibrium the length is 34 cm.

The bob is given a sharp tap so that it has an initial speed of 0.5 m s^{-1} downwards. If the greatest extension of the string is x cm, show that

$$x^2 - 8x + 6 = 0,$$

if g is taken as 10 m s^{-2}.

Find x and interpret the second solution of the quadratic equation.

8   Two climbers each of mass 70 kg have 20 m of rope between them when the higher one falls. At that moment he is 15 m above the second climber, who is firmly belayed to the rock face.

Find where the falling climber first comes to rest if he does not make contact with the rock face or his friend.

The rope stretches 1 m under a tension of 1000 N.

9   A bungee-jumper of mass 70 kg dives from a bridge 40 m above a river. The rope has unstretched length 28 m and elastic constant 580 N m^{-1}.

(a) Find the man's speed when the rope has length 37 m.

(b) Find the tension and the deceleration at this instant.

(c) Investigate what happens if the same rope is used with a jumper of mass 80 kg.

(d) Discuss some of the assumptions in the mathematical model.

B   Work and energy (answers p. 104)

In the last section the only forces that did work were weight and elastic forces. These were catered for by using the concept of gravitational potential energy and elastic potential energy.

When there are other forces like friction which do work, further terms must be included in energy equations.

Example 3

One end of a spring with constant 20 N m^{-1} is fixed, the other end is attached to a box of mass 0.5 kg. The box slides down a 20° slope with the spring parallel to the slope. Initially the spring is just unstretched. There is a friction force of 0.1 N.

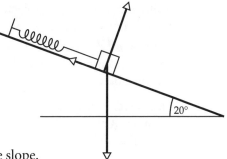

(a) Find how far the box goes down the slope.

(b) Find its greatest speed on the way down.

Solution

(a) PE is lost. Part of this is used to overcome friction, the rest is converted into EPE. The box gains KE then loses it all.

Suppose that it travels x metres.

$$\text{EPE gained} = \text{PE lost} - \text{work done by friction}$$

$$\Rightarrow \quad \tfrac{1}{2} \times 20 \times x^2 = 0.5g \times x \sin 20° - 0.1x$$

$$\Rightarrow \quad x = 0 \text{ or } 0.158$$

The box goes 0.16 m = 16 cm down the slope.

(b) When the box has moved y metres,

$$\text{KE gained} = \text{PE lost} - \text{EPE gained} - \text{work done by friction}$$

$$\Rightarrow \quad \tfrac{1}{2}mv^2 = 0.5g \times y \sin 20° - 10y^2 - 0.1y$$

This is a maximum when

$$0.5g \sin 20° - 20y - 0.1 = 0 \quad \text{(differentiating)}$$

$$y = 0.0788$$

Then $\quad \text{KE} = \tfrac{1}{2}0.5v^2 = 0.0621$

$$v = 0.498$$

The greatest speed is 0.50 ms^{-1}. It occurs when the acceleration is zero, i.e. the component of the weight down the slope equals the sum of the tension in the spring and the friction force. Note that this gives the equation above, and that $y = \tfrac{1}{2}x$.

Exercise B (answers p. 104)

1 A 7 kg mass lies on a rough table, the coefficient of friction being 0.5. It is attached to a point A, 3 m away, by a string of natural length 1.5 m. The mass is projected towards A with speed 4 m s^{-1} and reaches A with speed 2 m s^{-1}. Find the elastic constant of the string.

2 A sledge of mass 240 kg is pulled on level ground from rest by dogs with a total forward force of 150 N against a resistance of 45 N. How fast will the sledge be moving after it has gone 56 m?

3 A book of mass 0.3 kg is projected from a point A straight up a 20° slope at 3.5 m s^{-1}. It goes 1.2 m up the slope to B then returns to A.

Find the work done by friction during the motion from A to B. Will the same amount be done while returning to A? Find the speed with which the book returns to A.

4 A 2 kg parcel is projected up a 15° slope at 6 m s^{-1}. It returns to its starting point at 4 m s^{-1}. Find the total work done by friction and the distance that the parcel has travelled altogether.

5 A tile of mass 0.3 kg slides 4 m down a roof which slopes at 30° to the horizontal and then drops a further 6 m to the ground. The roof provides a friction force of 1 N. Find the speed with which the tile hits the ground.

6 One end of a string with elastic constant 6 N m^{-1} is attached to a fixed point A, the other to a bead of mass 20 grams. The bead is threaded on a straight horizontal wire which is 2 m from A. The bead is at rest at C with the string taut but unstretched. A force of 1 N is then applied in the direction of the wire.

Neglecting friction, find the speed when the bead has moved 1.5 m, and show that it is then slowing down at 40 m s^{-2}. Find also the initial acceleration.

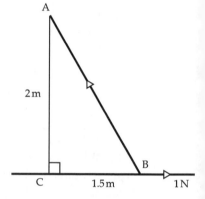

7 Two strings, each of unstretched length 17 cm and elastic constant 12 N m^{-1} are attached to a bob B of weight 0.64 N. The other ends are fixed at points P and Q which are at the same level and 30 cm apart.

The bob is released when it is 8 cm below R, the mid-point of PQ. Show that it comes to rest 20 cm below R. Find whether the bob is speeding up or slowing down when it is first 14 cm below R (i.e. half-way down).

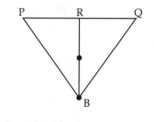

8 A small radio-controlled car of mass 0.1 kg is driven from rest 2 m along the flat then 2 m up a 20° slope and 2 m on the level again. It finally hits a wall at 1.6 m s^{-1}.

(a) Assuming a constant resistance force of 0.03 N, find the total energy taken from the battery.

(b) If this amount of energy was used while the car went 6 m from rest along a horizontal floor, what would be the final speed?

9 A parcel of mass 1 kg is given an initial speed of 2 m s^{-1} down a 10 m long chute sloping at 25° to the horizontal. At the bottom its speed is 3 m s^{-1}. Find the work done by friction and the coefficient of friction.

10 (a) Another parcel (of mass 1.4 kg) is placed on the chute of
question 9, with an initial speed of 5 m s^{-1}. The coefficient of
friction is 0.6. Find its speed at the bottom.

(b) If the parcel hits an identical parcel which is at rest 5 m down the
chute and the parcels then proceed together, find how far they go
before coming to rest.

11 A car of mass 1 tonne starts from rest on a level road. The propulsive
force is initially 4000 N, but this falls linearly with distance so that after
200 m its value is 700 N. There is a constant resistance force of 700 N.
Find the speed of the car after

(a) 100 m   (b) 200 m.

C Power (answers p. 105)

Power is defined in mathematics and physics as the rate of doing work.
This is, of course, equivalent to the rate of generating or using energy.

The unit of power is named after James Watt (1736–1819), the
Scottish inventor of the modern steam engine.

1 watt = 1 joule per second.

A 60 watt light bulb uses 60 joules of energy each second. A
lawnmower rated as 1 kW will do 1000 joules of work in 1 second.

Differentiating the various expressions for work done in one
dimension gives

$$\text{Power} = P = Fv.$$

This formula applies whether F is constant or not. The power
developed by a car engine has a maximum value. The expression Fv
confirms the well-known fact that the driving force (and hence the
ability to climb steep hills) is greater at slow speeds than higher speeds.

Example 4

A car of power 36 kW and mass 1000 kg (including the driver) has a
maximum speed of 4.5 m s^{-1} on a level road.

(a) Find the resistance to motion.

(b) Find the car's maximum speed up a $12\frac{1}{2}$% hill (1 in 8).

(c) Find the maximum speed up a $12\frac{1}{2}$% hill with passengers and
luggage totalling 300 kg.

Solution

(a) At maximum speed, driving force = resistance.

$$P = Fv \implies F = \frac{36 \times 10^3}{45} = 800$$

Hence the resistance = 800 N

(b) Resolving forces along the slope,

$$F = 800 + \frac{1000g}{8}, \text{ assuming unchanged resistance.}$$

Maximum speed $= \dfrac{36 \times 10^3}{F} = 18 \text{ m s}^{-1}$

(c) $F = 800 + \dfrac{1300g}{8} \Rightarrow v = 15 \text{ m s}^{-1}$

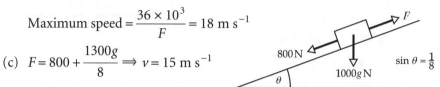

Exercise C (answers p. 105)

1   A car of mass 1100 kg can accelerate from 15 m s^{-1} to 35 m s^{-1} in
    9.3 s. Find the gain in KE and the average power of the engine. Ignore
    resistance forces.

2   A pump takes water from rest in a hole in the road and delivers it 2 m
    higher on the road surface at 3 m s^{-1} at a flow rate of 25 kg s^{-1}. If the
    pump is 80% efficient, find the power required to drive the pump.

3   A pump is required to fill a swimming pool from a reservoir 20 m
    below the pump outlet. The pool is 25 m by 10 m and slopes
    uniformly from a depth of 1 m to a depth of 2.4 m. The filling process
    must take less than 8 hours. Find the minimum power of the pump
    assuming that it is 70% efficient. Comment on the assumptions made.
    (1 m^3 of water has a mass of 1000 kg.)

4   A man steadily winds up the 2 kg 'weight' of a grandfather clock
    through 1.5 m in $\frac{1}{4}$ minute. Find the power of the tension in the chain
    over the weight. Is the power of the force between the man's finger and
    the key likely to be larger than this?

5   A car has mass 1.2 tonnes and maximum power 60 kW. Assume a
    resistance to motion of 1400 N throughout.
    (a) Find the maximum acceleration on a level road when travelling at
         30 m s^{-1}.
    (b) Find the maximum speed up a hill with gradient 1 in 20.
    (c) Find the power developed when the car is driven up a 1 in 20 hill
         at a steady 20 m s^{-1}.

6   A cyclist working at 2 kW has a maximum speed of 6 m s^{-1} up a
    1 in 15 slope. The total mass of cycle and cyclist is 90 kg.
    (a) Find the total resistance force.
    (b) Find the maximum speed down a 1 in 15 slope working at 1.5 kW
         if the resistance is unchanged.

7 A train of mass 450 tonnes has a maximum speed of 40 m s^{-1} on the level. The total resistance force is 140 kN.

   (a) Find the power of the engine.

   (b) Assuming the same power and resistance, find the maximum speed up a gradient of 1 in 120.

8 (a) A crane steadily raises a $7\frac{1}{2}$ tonne ingot at a rate of 2 m s^{-1}. Find the power of the force at the attachment. Is the power of the force on the chain at the drum likely to be larger than this?

   (b) If the power of the force at the axle of the drum is increased to 240 kW and the power of the force at the point of attachment is 70% of this, what will be the acceleration of the ingot when the speed is 2 m s^{-1}?

   (c) If the crane continues to produce this power, what will be the final steady speed achieved by the ingot?

9E (a) Show that $\dfrac{d}{dt}(Fx) = Fv$ if F is constant.

   (b) Show that $\dfrac{d}{dt}(\tfrac{1}{2}mv^2) = Fv$.

   (c) For a variable force F in one dimension,

$$\text{work done} = \text{WD} = \int F\,dx.$$

    Show that $\dfrac{d}{dt}(\text{WD}) = Fv$.

After working through this chapter you should

1 know that kinetic energy (KE), gravitational potential energy (PE) and elastic potential energy (EPE) are all forms of mechanical energy

2 know that the total work done by all other forces on a body is equal to the change in the total mechanical energy

3 know that power is the rate of doing work or the rate of change of energy

4 know that

       1 watt = 1 joule per second

5 know that the power of a force F is given by Fv where v is the velocity.

8 Impulse and work in two dimensions

A Constant forces (answers p. 106)

You have seen that for motion in a straight line, the equation $F = ma$ can be integrated to give

$$\int F\,dt = mv - mu.$$

The left-hand side is the impulse of the resultant force, the right-hand side is the change in momentum. If F is constant, the impulse is Ft.

You know that for motion in two (or three) dimensions, Newton's second law is expressed as

$$\mathbf{F} = m\mathbf{a} = m\frac{d\mathbf{v}}{dt}$$

Integration gives $\mathbf{F}t = m\mathbf{v} - m\mathbf{u}$ for constant $\mathbf{F}$. The minus sign indicates *vector* subtraction. The impulse and the two velocities may be in different directions. A familiar example is a projectile.

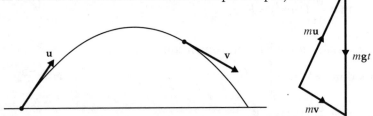

The vector triangle shows how the impulse due to the weight relates to the momentum vectors.

Example 1

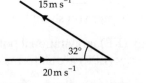

A hockey ball of mass 0.15 kg is moving at 20 m s^{-1} when it is hit, changing its velocity to 15 m s^{-1} in the direction shown. Find the magnitude and direction of the impulse

(a) by drawing

(b) using components.

Solution

Scale: 1 cm = 1 N s

(a) $mu = 0.15 \times 20 = 3$ N s

$mv = 0.15 \times 15 = 2.25$ N s

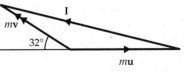

The magnitude and direction of the impulse can be taken from the diagram.

(b) $m\mathbf{u} = \begin{bmatrix} 3 \\ 0 \end{bmatrix}$, $m\mathbf{v} = \begin{bmatrix} -2.25\cos 32° \\ 2.25\sin 32° \end{bmatrix} = \begin{bmatrix} -1.91 \\ 1.19 \end{bmatrix}$

$$m\mathbf{v} - m\mathbf{u} = \begin{bmatrix} -1.91 \\ 1.19 \end{bmatrix} - \begin{bmatrix} 3 \\ 0 \end{bmatrix} = \begin{bmatrix} -4.91 \\ 1.19 \end{bmatrix}$$

$$= 5.05 \text{ N s at } 166.4° \text{ to the } x\text{-direction.}$$

How can we express the work done by a constant force using vectors?

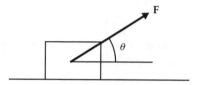

Suppose a body is moved a distance r along the floor by the force $\mathbf{F}$ shown.

The work done $= F\cos\theta \times r$

This is the scalar product $\mathbf{F} \cdot \mathbf{r}$ where $\mathbf{r}$ is the displacement vector. This applies even when the motion is not in a straight line.

When a child goes down this slide, the displacement vector is as shown.

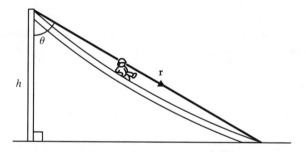

The work done by the weight $= m\mathbf{g} \cdot \mathbf{r} = mgr\cos\theta = mgh$. This is consistent with all you have done in earlier chapters.

You should know that $(\mathbf{a} + \mathbf{b}) \cdot \mathbf{c} = \mathbf{a} \cdot \mathbf{c} + \mathbf{b} \cdot \mathbf{c}$ for any three vectors $\mathbf{a}, \mathbf{b}, \mathbf{c}$.

We can interpret the version $(\mathbf{P} + \mathbf{Q}) \cdot \mathbf{r} = \mathbf{P} \cdot \mathbf{r} + \mathbf{Q} \cdot \mathbf{r}$ as saying

> When a body undergoes a displacement $\mathbf{r}$, the work done by the resultant of two forces $\mathbf{P}$ and $\mathbf{Q}$ acting on it is equal to the sum of the work done by $\mathbf{P}$ and the work done by $\mathbf{Q}$.

This will come as no surprise.

Now let us see what happens when the vectors are written in component form.

You know that a force $\mathbf{F} = \begin{bmatrix} a \\ b \end{bmatrix}$ can be replaced by

component forces $\mathbf{a} = \begin{bmatrix} a \\ 0 \end{bmatrix}$ and $\mathbf{b} = \begin{bmatrix} 0 \\ b \end{bmatrix}$ as shown.

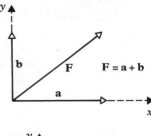

Similarly, a displacement $\mathbf{r} = \begin{bmatrix} c \\ d \end{bmatrix}$ can be written as

$\mathbf{r} = \mathbf{c} + \mathbf{d}$ where $\mathbf{c} = \begin{bmatrix} c \\ 0 \end{bmatrix}$ and $\mathbf{d} = \begin{bmatrix} 0 \\ d \end{bmatrix}$.

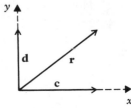

So $\mathbf{F} \cdot \mathbf{r} = (\mathbf{a} + \mathbf{b}) \cdot (\mathbf{c} + \mathbf{d})$
$= \mathbf{a} \cdot \mathbf{c} + \mathbf{a} \cdot \mathbf{d} + \mathbf{b} \cdot \mathbf{c} + \mathbf{b} \cdot \mathbf{d}$
$= ac \cos 0° + ad \cos 90° + bc \cos 90° + bd \cos 0°$
$= ac + bd$

> When a force $\mathbf{F} = \begin{bmatrix} a \\ b \end{bmatrix}$ moves its point of application a distance
>
> $\mathbf{r} = \begin{bmatrix} x \\ y \end{bmatrix}$ then the work done by the force is
>
> $$\mathbf{F} \cdot \mathbf{r} = \begin{bmatrix} a \\ b \end{bmatrix} \cdot \begin{bmatrix} x \\ y \end{bmatrix} = ax + by$$

That is, the value of the work done is obtained by first multiplying the corresponding elements together and then summing the results.

Example 2

A particle is acted upon by two forces, $\begin{bmatrix} 3 \\ 4 \end{bmatrix}$ and $\begin{bmatrix} 5 \\ -12 \end{bmatrix}$ newtons. If it is

displaced through $\begin{bmatrix} 16 \\ -16 \end{bmatrix}$ metres, find the work done by each of the forces.

Solution

Work done by the $\begin{bmatrix} 3 \\ 4 \end{bmatrix}$ force is

$\begin{bmatrix} 3 \\ 4 \end{bmatrix} \cdot \begin{bmatrix} 16 \\ -16 \end{bmatrix} = 48 + -64 = -16$ joules

Work done by the $\begin{bmatrix} 5 \\ -12 \end{bmatrix}$ force is

$\begin{bmatrix} 5 \\ -12 \end{bmatrix} \cdot \begin{bmatrix} 16 \\ -16 \end{bmatrix} = 80 + 192 = 272$ joules

Exercise A (answers p. 106)

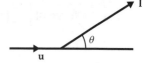

1 A ball of mass 0.15 kg travelling at 20 m s^{-1} is given an impulse **I** at an angle θ to the original direction of motion.

Find the velocity **v** after impact when

(a) $I = 6$ N s, $\theta = 180°$

(b) $I = 3$ N s, $\theta = 180°$

(c) $I = 3$ N s, $\theta = 120°$

(d) $I = 5$ N s, $\theta = 160°$

2 A cricket ball of mass 0.15 kg travelling at 30 m s^{-1} is hit through the slips. It is deflected through 50° and the speed is reduced to 25 m s^{-1}. Find the impulse, assuming both velocities are horizontal.

3 A force of 5 newtons acts on a particle at A, which is displaced 4 metres along AB.

(a) Calculate the work done by the force.

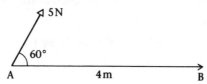

(b) If the direction of the force is reversed but the displacement remains the same, i.e. $\overrightarrow{AB}$, calculate the work done by this new force.

4 Calculate the scalar product of the following pairs of vectors.

(a)

8

64°

3

(b)

2

9

155°

(c)

2

25°

9

5 A roller is pulled 7 metres across a cricket pitch. The handle is pulled with a force of 100 newtons at an angle of 70° to the vertical.

(a) What is the work done by this force?

(b) What is the work done if the handle is pushed with the same force?

6 A horse pulls a barge of mass 30 tonnes along a canal by means of a rope which makes an angle of 20° with the direction of the barge.

If the tension in the rope is 200 newtons, find the work done by this force in pulling the barge 1 km.

7 Find the work done when a force **F** newtons acts on a particle which subsequently moves through a displacement **r** metres where

(a) $\mathbf{F} = \begin{bmatrix} 2 \\ 4 \end{bmatrix}$, $\mathbf{r} = \begin{bmatrix} 12 \\ -4 \end{bmatrix}$ (b) $\mathbf{F} = \begin{bmatrix} 1 \\ -2 \end{bmatrix}$, $\mathbf{r} = \begin{bmatrix} -3 \\ 4 \end{bmatrix}$

8   A force of $\begin{bmatrix} 3 \\ -5 \end{bmatrix}$ newtons acts on a particle moving parallel to the vector

$\begin{bmatrix} 5 \\ 12 \end{bmatrix}$. If the work done by the force is 90 joules, what is the distance

travelled?

9   Forces of $\begin{bmatrix} 3 \\ -3 \end{bmatrix}$ and $\begin{bmatrix} 9 \\ 15 \end{bmatrix}$ newtons act on a particle. If its displacement is

parallel to the resultant of the two forces and the total work done by
both forces is 120 joules, find the displacement.

10   A particle of mass 10 grams is initially moving with velocity $\begin{bmatrix} 4 \\ 16 \end{bmatrix}$ m s^{-1}.

Two seconds later, its velocity is $\begin{bmatrix} 8 \\ -20 \end{bmatrix}$ m s^{-1}.

Calculate the impulse and the work that has been done on the particle.

11   A force of $\begin{bmatrix} 6 \\ 5 \end{bmatrix}$ newtons moves a body of mass 0.2 kg from A $(7, 8)$

to B $(10, 12)$.

(a) Calculate the work done by the force.

(b) If the body starts from rest, what is its speed at B?

B Variable forces (answers p. 107)

For forces which vary with time,

$$\mathbf{F} = m\mathbf{a} \quad \Rightarrow \quad \int \mathbf{F}\,dt = m\mathbf{v} - m\mathbf{u}$$

Example 3

A force $\mathbf{F} = \begin{bmatrix} 10t \\ 6t^2 \end{bmatrix}$ acts on a body of mass 10 from $t = 0$ to $t = 2$. The

initial velocity is $\begin{bmatrix} 1 \\ 3 \end{bmatrix}$. Find the impulse, the final velocity and the

change in kinetic energy.

Solution

$$\text{Impulse} = \int_0^2 \mathbf{F}\,dt = \begin{bmatrix} 5t^2 \\ 2t^3 \end{bmatrix} \text{ from } t = 0 \text{ to } t = 2$$

$$= \begin{bmatrix} 20 \\ 16 \end{bmatrix}$$

Change in momentum = impulse $\Rightarrow 10\mathbf{v} - 10 \begin{bmatrix} 1 \\ 3 \end{bmatrix} = \begin{bmatrix} 20 \\ 16 \end{bmatrix}$

$$\Rightarrow \qquad \mathbf{v} = \begin{bmatrix} 3 \\ 4.6 \end{bmatrix}$$

The final speed $= \sqrt{3^2 + 4.6^2}$; final KE $= \frac{1}{2} \times 10 \times (3^2 + 4.6^2)$
$$= 150.8$$

Similarly the initial KE = 50

Energy is a scalar (non-vector) quantity. The change is
$150.8 - 50 = 100.8$.

No units are mentioned in this example.

> The impulse provided by a variable force $\mathbf{F}$ is $\displaystyle\int \mathbf{F}\,dt$ taken between appropriate limits.

What is the formula for the work done by a variable force in two or three dimensions? An example will show us.

The position vector of a particle of mass m at time t is given by

$$\mathbf{r} = \begin{bmatrix} -3t^2 + 8t \\ t^3 \end{bmatrix}.$$

We can write down $\mathbf{v} = \begin{bmatrix} -6t + 8 \\ 3t^2 \end{bmatrix}, \quad \mathbf{a} = \begin{bmatrix} -6 \\ 6t \end{bmatrix}.$

A plot of the path of the particle from $t = 0$ to $t = 2$ is shown. The values of $\mathbf{v}$ are consistent with this.

At time t, KE $= \frac{1}{2}m[(-6t + 8)^2 + (3t^2)^2]$

Using the chain rule with this expression unsimplified gives

$$\frac{d}{dt}(\text{KE}) = m[(-6)(-6t + 8) + (6t)(3t^2)]$$

You can recognise the expression in the square bracket as a scalar product:

$$\frac{d}{dt}(\text{KE}) = m\mathbf{a} \cdot \mathbf{v}$$

$$= \mathbf{F} \cdot \mathbf{v}$$

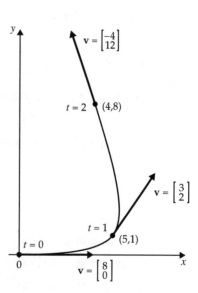

This is the expression you would expect for the power in two dimensions. It follows immediately that

$$\text{change in KE} = \int \mathbf{F} \cdot \mathbf{v} \, dt.$$

This is the most general form for the work done by a force.

For motion in two or three dimensions, the power of a force $\mathbf{F}$ acting on a body moving with velocity $\mathbf{v}$ is

$$\mathbf{F} \cdot \mathbf{v},$$

and the work done is

$$\int \mathbf{F} \cdot \mathbf{v} \, dt.$$

Example 4

At time t seconds, a body of mass 4 kg has position vector (in metres) given by

$$\mathbf{r} = \begin{bmatrix} t^3 + 3t \\ 2t^2 + 5t \end{bmatrix}.$$

Find expressions for the velocity, acceleration and force vectors in terms of t. Find also the power and the work done between $t = 0$ and $t = 2$.

Solution

By differentiation, $\mathbf{v} = \begin{bmatrix} 3t^2 + 3 \\ 4t + 5 \end{bmatrix}$, $\mathbf{a} = \begin{bmatrix} 6t \\ 4 \end{bmatrix}$

$$\mathbf{F} = m\mathbf{a} = 4 \begin{bmatrix} 6t \\ 4 \end{bmatrix} = \begin{bmatrix} 24t \\ 16 \end{bmatrix}$$

$$\begin{aligned} P = \mathbf{F} \cdot \mathbf{v} &= 24t(3t^2 + 3) + 16(4t + 5) \\ &= 72t^3 + 136t + 80 \end{aligned}$$

Between $t = 0$ and $t = 2$, $\text{WD} = \int_0^2 P \, dt$

$$= \left[18t^4 + 68t^2 + 80t \right]_0^2$$

$$= 720$$

The work done is 720 J.

Note that at $t = 0$, $\text{KE} = \frac{1}{2} \times 4 \times (3^2 + 5^2) = 68$ J

At $t = 2$, $\text{KE} = \frac{1}{2} \times 4 \times (15^2 + 13^2) = 788$ J

$$\begin{aligned} \text{WD by } \mathbf{F} = \text{change of KE} &= 788 - 68 \\ &= 720 \text{ J} \end{aligned}$$

Instead of writing $\begin{bmatrix} 3 \\ 5 \end{bmatrix}$, say, an alternative notation is $3\mathbf{i} + 5\mathbf{j}$, where $\mathbf{i}$ and $\mathbf{j}$ are unit vectors in the x and y directions. Some books write vectors in this way, some in the column vector way. Here is a worked example like Example 4 written using the $\mathbf{i}, \mathbf{j}$ notation.

Example 5

A body of mass 3 kg is acted upon by a force $\mathbf{F}$ newtons.
At time t seconds, $\mathbf{F} = 9t^2\mathbf{i} + (4t - 2)\mathbf{j}$. When $t = 0$, the velocity is $\mathbf{i} + 3\mathbf{j}$.
Find the work done between $t = 1$ and $t = 3$.

Solution

$\mathbf{F} = m\mathbf{a}$ gives $\mathbf{a} = 3t^2\mathbf{i} + \frac{1}{3}(4t - 2)\mathbf{j}$
Integration gives $\mathbf{v} = t^3\mathbf{i} + \frac{1}{3}(2t^2 - 2t)\mathbf{j} + \mathbf{c}$,
where $\mathbf{c} = \mathbf{i} + 3\mathbf{j}$, the initial velocity.
So $\mathbf{v} = (t^3 + 1)\mathbf{i} + (\frac{2}{3}t^2 - \frac{2}{3}t + 3)\mathbf{j}$
When $t = 3$, $\mathbf{v} = 28\mathbf{i} + 7\mathbf{j}$;
When $t = 1$, $\mathbf{v} = 2\mathbf{i} + 3\mathbf{j}$.
Work done = change in KE
$$= \tfrac{1}{2} \times 3 \times [(28^2 + 7^2) - (2^2 + 3^2)]$$
$$= 1230 \text{ J}$$

Exercise B (answers p. 107)

1   Find the impulses provided by the following forces over the given time intervals.

(a) $\mathbf{F} = \begin{bmatrix} -2t \\ 3 \end{bmatrix}$ from $t = 0$ to $t = 3$

(b) $\mathbf{F} = \begin{bmatrix} \sin t \\ \cos t \end{bmatrix}$ from $t = 0$ to $t = \frac{1}{2}\pi$

(c) $\mathbf{F} = \begin{bmatrix} e^t \\ t \end{bmatrix}$ from $t = 0$ to $t = 1$.

2   Show that in Example 3,
$$\mathbf{F} \cdot \mathbf{v} = 10t + 18t^2 + 5t^3 + 1.2t^5$$

at time t.

Use this expression to check that the change in KE between $t = 0$ and $t = 2$ is 100.8 units.

3 A radio-controlled toy car of mass
0.05 kg is driven round a figure of eight
track. At time t seconds its position
vector (in metres) is

$$\mathbf{r} = \begin{bmatrix} \sin t \\ 0.6 \sin 2t \end{bmatrix}.$$

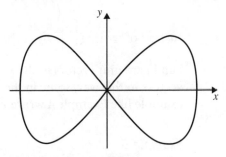

(a) Find the position, velocity and acceleration when $t = 1$. Show these
on a copy of the diagram and check that your answers are sensible.

(b) Find the impulse and the work done on the car from $t = 0$ to $t = 1$.

4 A particle of mass m has position vector $\mathbf{r}$ at time t. Find the velocity,
acceleration and force vectors, given

(a) $m = 2, \mathbf{r} = \begin{bmatrix} e^t \\ e^{-t} \end{bmatrix}$

(b) $m = 5, \mathbf{r} = 3 \sin t\,\mathbf{i} + 5 \cos t\,\mathbf{j}$

(c) $m = 4, \mathbf{r} = (t+1)^2\mathbf{i} + (t-1)^2\mathbf{j}$

In each case find the impulse and the work done between $t = 0$ and $t = 1$.

5 Show that when $\mathbf{a}$ and $\mathbf{b}$ are both vector functions of t,

$$\frac{d}{dt}(\mathbf{a} \cdot \mathbf{b}) = \frac{d\mathbf{a}}{dt} \cdot \mathbf{b} + \mathbf{a} \cdot \frac{d\mathbf{b}}{dt}.$$

Deduce that $\dfrac{d}{dt}(\tfrac{1}{2}m\mathbf{v} \cdot \mathbf{v}) = \mathbf{F} \cdot \mathbf{v}$.

After working through this chapter you should

1 know that impulse is given most generally by $\displaystyle\int \mathbf{F}\,dt$, which simplifies to

(a) $\mathbf{F}t$ for constant $\mathbf{F}$

(b) $\displaystyle\int F\,dt$ (represented by the area under the (t, F) graph) for a
variable force in one dimension

2 know that work done is given most generally by $\displaystyle\int \mathbf{F} \cdot \mathbf{v}\,dt$, which
simplifies to

(a) $\mathbf{F} \cdot \mathbf{r}$ for a constant force in two dimensions

(b) Fx for a constant force in one dimension

(c) $\displaystyle\int F\,dx$ (represented by the area under the (x, F) graph) for a
variable force in one dimension

3 know that power is given most generally by $\mathbf{F} \cdot \mathbf{v}$, which simplifies to
Fv in one dimension.

Answers

1 Work and kinetic energy

A Speed and distance (p. 1)

1 Plotting a (u, x) graph with these values produces a shape as shown.

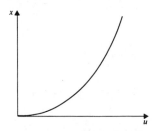

When u is doubled (from 40 to 80), x is multiplied by 4 (from 9 to 36). This suggests that x is proportional to u^2.

Trying pairs of values for u and x shows that the relationship appears to be approximately

$x = 0.0056u^2$

When $u = 120$, $x = 81$.

For an initial speed of 120 km h^{-1}, the skid marks may be expected to be of length about 80 metres.

2 (a) 10 m s^{-1} (b) 2.81 m, 12.5 m s^{-1}
 (c) 12.5 m s^{-1}

3 $v^2 = u^2 + 2gh$; no difference

4 $v^2 = u^2 + 2ax$
 $\Rightarrow \frac{1}{2}mv^2 = \frac{1}{2}mu^2 + max$
 $\Rightarrow \frac{1}{2}mv^2 = \frac{1}{2}mu^2 + Fx$

5 It appears that the friction force in question 1 is constant since x is approximately proportional to u^2. Question 4 predicts this when $v = 0$.

6 Chemical, nuclear, light, sound, magnetic.

Chemical or nuclear energy is converted into heat and then electricity in a power station.

Electrical energy is converted into mechanical energy in an electric motor.

Chemical energy is converted into mechanical energy in a car or when riding a bicycle.

Exercise A (p. 3)

1 1.2×10^6 J; 1.2×10^4 N

2 The resistive force, F newtons, is given by

$F \times 0.02 =$
 $\qquad \frac{1}{2} \times 0.015 \times 300^2 - \frac{1}{2} \times 0.015 \times 500^2$
 $\Rightarrow \quad F = -6 \times 10^4$

The resistive force has magnitude 6×10^4 newtons.

3 The accelerating force, F newtons, is given by

$F \times 15 = 1000 \times 108 \times \frac{1000}{3600}$
 $\Rightarrow \quad F = 2000$
The accelerating force is 2000 newtons.

The distance travelled while accelerating, x metres, is given by

$2000x = \frac{1}{2} \times 1000 \times (108 \times \frac{1000}{3600})^2$
 $\Rightarrow \quad x = 225$

The distance travelled while slowing down, y metres, is given by

$-500y = \frac{1}{2} \times 1000 \times 0^2 - \frac{1}{2} \times 1000$
 $\qquad\qquad\qquad\qquad \times (108 \times \frac{1000}{3600})^2$
 $\Rightarrow \quad y = 900$

The total distance travelled is 1125 metres.

4 The speed attained is 20 m s^{-1}. In reality, the force would vary in each gear.

5 50 km h^{-1} = 13.89 m s^{-1}

The initial sliding speed of the van, u m s^{-1}, is given by

$-2 \times 10^4 \times 32 = \frac{1}{2} \times 2250 \times 13.89^2$
 $\qquad\qquad\qquad\qquad -\frac{1}{2} \times 2250 \times u^2$
 $\Rightarrow \qquad\qquad u = 27.6$

The initial sliding speed of the van was around 27.6 m s^{-1}.

$27.6 \times \frac{3600}{1000} = 99.4$ km h^{-1}

The type of skid test described would be extremely unreliable and potentially inaccurate.

6 Circumference of (assumed circular) orbit

$$= 2 \times \pi \times 1.5 \times 10^8 \times 10^3 \text{ metres}$$
$$= 3\pi \times 10^{11} \text{ metres}$$

Speed of the Earth relative to the Sun

$$= \frac{3\pi \times 10^{11}}{365 \times 24 \times 60 \times 60} \text{ m s}^{-1}$$
$$\approx 2.99 \times 10^4 \text{ m s}^{-1}$$

Kinetic energy of the Earth

$$= \tfrac{1}{2} \times 6.04 \times 10^{24} \times 2.99^2 \times 10^8 \text{ J}$$
$$\approx 3 \times 10^{33} \text{ J (to 1 s.f.)}$$

7 7 m s^{-1}

8 (a) 39 m   (b) 62 m

9 5.2 N

B Potential energy (p. 4)

Exercise B (p. 6)

1 The height above the ground is 2 metres.

⟹ gravitational potential energy relative to the ground $= 5 \times 10 \times 2$
$$= 100 \text{ joules}$$

2 Height of the child above the ground

$$= 5 \sin 36° = 2.94 \text{ metres}$$

Gravitational PE relative to the ground

$$= 882 \text{ joules}$$

3 4900 J

4 (a)

(i)   Height of top of ramp
$$= 34.4 \sin 5°$$
$$= 3.00 \text{ metres}$$

Work done by gravity
$$= -500 \times 3.00$$
$$= -1500 \text{ joules}$$

(ii) Height of top of ramp
$$= 8.0 \sin 22°$$
$$= 3.00 \text{ metres}$$

Work done by gravity
$$= -500 \times 3.00$$
$$= -1500 \text{ joules}$$

(b) The height the hod is lifted through is the same in each case.

5 Height of top of ladder above ground

$$= l \sin 70°$$

Increase in PE $= 50 \times 10 \times l \sin 70°$

But the increase $= 4300$ J

⟹ $500 l \sin 70° = 4300$
$$l = 9.15 \text{ metres}$$

C Conserving energy (p. 6)

1 (a) $70 g \sin \theta$; $g \sin \theta$

(b) $\dfrac{h}{\sin \theta}$; $v^2 = u^2 + 2gh$

(c) No; no

(d) Yes

2 (a) 18.4 m s^{-1} (b) 18.4 m s^{-1}

Exercise C (p. 9)

1 (a) PE relative to initial position $= 0.2 \times 3$
$$= 0.6 \text{ J}$$

(b) KE at the start
$$= \tfrac{1}{2} \times 0.02 \times 15^2 = 2.25 \text{ J}$$
KE + PE at start $=$ KE + PE after 3 metres
⟹ $\tfrac{1}{2} mv^2 + 0.6 = 2.25 + 0$
$$v = 12.8 \text{ m s}^{-1}$$

(c) At the highest point of its path, the kinetic energy of the ball is zero.

By conservation of energy,

PE at the highest point $+ 0 = 0 + 2.25$
PE $= 2.25$ joules

2

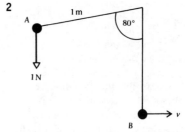

PE at A relative to B

$$= 0.1 \times 10 \times 1(1 - \cos 80°)$$
$$= 0.826 \text{ joules}$$

KE at A $= 0$

But KE + PE at A $=$ KE + PE at B
⟹ $0 + 0.826 = \tfrac{1}{2} \times 0.1 \times v^2 + 0$
$$v = 4.06 \text{ m s}^{-1}$$

3 **(a)** Assume conservation of mechanical energy as the lighter ball bearing swings down.

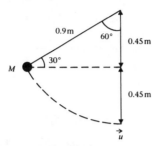

KE gained = PE lost

$$\Rightarrow \quad \tfrac{1}{2}Mu^2 = Mgh$$
$$\tfrac{1}{2}u^2 = 10 \times 0.45$$
$$\Rightarrow \quad u^2 = 9$$
$$\Rightarrow \quad u = 3 \text{ m s}^{-1}$$

(b) Momentum is conserved in the collision.

Before impact   **After impact**

The momentum is $3M + 0 = 3Mv$

$$\Rightarrow \quad v = 1 \text{ m s}^{-1}$$

(c) Assume conservation of mechanical energy as the combined mass swings up.

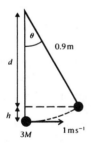

KE lost = PE gained

$$\Rightarrow \quad \tfrac{1}{2} \times 3M \times 1^2 = 3M \times 10 \times h$$
$$h = 0.05 \text{ metre}$$
$$\Rightarrow \quad d = 0.85 \text{ metre}$$
$$\Rightarrow \quad \theta = \cos^{-1}\left(\frac{0.85}{0.9}\right)$$
$$= 19°$$

4 Loss of PE = $30g \times 10 \approx 3000$ J

Gain of KE = $\tfrac{1}{2} \times 30 \times 4^2 = 240$ J

Work done by friction = 2760 J

5 **(a)** $\tfrac{1}{2}mv^2 - \tfrac{1}{2}m \times 9 = mg \times 1$
$$\Rightarrow \qquad v^2 = 29$$
$$\Rightarrow \qquad v = 5.4 \text{ m s}^{-1}$$

(b) $mgh' = \tfrac{1}{2}m \times 29$
$$\Rightarrow \quad h' = 1.45$$

Her maximum height is 1.45 m above the bottom point, i.e. 2.45 m above the ground.

(c) No, you do not need to know her mass.

6 **(a)** Assume the Scout starts from rest and that $g = 10$ m s^{-2}. Assume there is no friction. Ignore the extra sag due to the Scout's weight.

$$\tfrac{1}{2}mv^2 = mg \times 8 \quad \Rightarrow \quad v = 12.6 \text{ m s}^{-1}$$

(b) $v = 11.0$ m s^{-1}

(c) The final speed is too great. The runway is unsafe.

7 19.0 m s^{-1}

8 $\sin^{-1} 0.2 = 11.5°$

9 25 000 J

The source is the chemical energy stored in her body.

10 **(a)** $60g \times 30 = 18\,000$ J
(b) $\tfrac{1}{2} \times 60 \times (100 - 36) = 1920$ J
(c) $18\,000 - 1920 \approx 16\,000$ J

Some work is done by friction in the wheel hubs. Air resistance also helps to slow the cycle down. These have been ignored.

11 **(a)** $\tfrac{1}{2} \times 3.1 \times 4.2^2 = 27.34$ J = 27 J (to 2 s.f.)
(b) $3.1 \times 10 \times 1.6 \sin 20° = 16.96$ J
$$= 17 \text{ J (to 2 s.f.)}$$
(c) $27.34 - 16.96 = 10.38$ J = 10 J (to 2 s.f.)
(d) $10.38 \div 1.6 = 6.49$ N = 6.5 N (to 2 s.f.)
(e) $6.49 \div (3.1 \times 10 \times \cos 20°) = 0.22$
$$\text{(to 2 s.f.)}$$

12 PE gained = $650g \times 15$
$$= 97\,550 \text{ J}$$

KE gained = $\tfrac{1}{2} \times 650 \times (30^2 - 18^2)$
$$= 187\,200 \text{ J}$$

WD by engine = $(97\,550 + 187\,200) \div 0.9$

$$\approx 3.2 \times 10^5 \text{ J}$$

13E $\mathbf{a} = \begin{bmatrix} 0 \\ -g \end{bmatrix} \Rightarrow \mathbf{v} = \begin{bmatrix} a \\ b - gt \end{bmatrix} \Rightarrow \mathbf{r} = \begin{bmatrix} at \\ bt - \frac{1}{2}gt^2 \end{bmatrix}$

$U^2 = a^2 + b^2, \quad h = bt - \frac{1}{2}gt^2$

$\begin{aligned} V^2 &= a^2 + (b - gt)^2 \\ &= a^2 + b^2 - 2bgt + g^2 t^2 \\ &= (a^2 + b^2) - 2g(bt - \frac{1}{2}gt^2) \\ &= U^2 - 2gh \end{aligned}$

Hence $\frac{1}{2}mV^2 = \frac{1}{2}mU^2 - mgh$

2 Momentum and energy

A Collisions (p. 12)

1D The sound energy must come from some loss of kinetic energy.

2D (a) Total momentum $= 6 \times 5 + 4 \times 2$
        $= 38 \text{ kg ms}^{-1}$
    Total KE $= \frac{1}{2} \times 6 \times 5^2 + \frac{1}{2} \times 4 \times 2^2$
        $= 83 \text{ J}$

(b) Speed of Q $= (38 - 6 \times 3) \div 4 = 5 \text{ m s}^{-1}$
    New total KE $= \frac{1}{2} \times 6 \times 3^2 + \frac{1}{2} \times 4 \times 5^2$
        $= 77 \text{ J}$

Exercise A (p. 13)

1 Speed $= \frac{2}{3} \text{ m s}^{-1}$
    Original KE $= 540 \text{ J}$
    Final KE $= 307 \text{ J}$
    Loss of KE $= 233 \text{ J}$

2 Speed $= 4.25 \text{ m s}^{-1}$
    Loss of KE $= 150 \text{ J}$

3 Mass $= 0.14 \text{ kg}$
    Loss of KE $= 0.066 \text{ J}$

4 0.15 m s^{-1} in the original direction
    Loss of KE $= 135 \text{ J}$

5

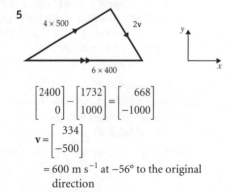

$\begin{bmatrix} 2400 \\ 0 \end{bmatrix} - \begin{bmatrix} 1732 \\ 1000 \end{bmatrix} = \begin{bmatrix} 668 \\ -1000 \end{bmatrix}$

$\mathbf{v} = \begin{bmatrix} 334 \\ -500 \end{bmatrix}$

$= 600 \text{ m s}^{-1}$ at $-56°$ to the original direction

KE gain $= 3.8 \times 10^5 \text{ J}$

6 Satellite: 9600 m s^{-1} at $4.8°$
    Nose-cone: $16\,000 \text{ m s}^{-1}$ at $53.1°$
    Gain in KE $= 1.1 \times 10^9 \text{ J}$

7 Momentum: $0.197 \text{ kg m s}^{-1}$, $0.118 \text{ kg m s}^{-1}$
    Speed: 1.97 m s^{-1}, 1.18 m s^{-1}
    KE lost $= 0.25 \text{ J}$

B Perfectly elastic collisions (p. 14)

Exercise B (p. 15)

1

		Before collision	After collision
(a)	(i)	mu	mu
	(ii)	$\frac{1}{2}mu^2$	$\frac{1}{2}mu^2$
	(iii)	Speed of approach $= u$	Speed of separation $= u$
(b)	(i)	$2mu$	$\frac{2}{3}mu + \frac{4}{3}mu$ $= 2mu$
	(ii)	mu^2	$\frac{1}{9}mu^2 + \frac{8}{9}mu^2$ $= mu^2$
	(iii)	u	$\frac{4}{3}u - \frac{1}{3}u = u$
(c)	(i)	mu	$-\frac{1}{3}mu + \frac{4}{3}mu$ $= mu$
	(ii)	$\frac{1}{2}mu^2$	$\frac{1}{18}mu^2 + \frac{4}{9}mu^2$ $= \frac{1}{2}mu^2$
	(iii)	u	$\frac{2}{3}u - (-\frac{1}{3}u) = u$

2 (a) Let the speed of one truck after the collision be w.

Before collision   **After collision**

$\boxed{m} \!\to\! v \; v \!\leftarrow\! \boxed{m} \qquad \boxed{m} \!\to\! w \; \boxed{m} \!\to\! w + 2$

Speed of separation = speed of approach
        $= 2v$

So the speed of the other truck after the collision is $w + 2v$.

Since momentum is conserved,
$$mv - mv = mw + m(w + 2v)$$
$$\Rightarrow \quad 0 = w + w + 2v$$
$$\Rightarrow \quad w = -v$$
$$\Rightarrow \quad w + 2v = -v + 2v = v$$

The velocities of the two trucks after collision are as shown. $v \!\leftarrow\! \boxed{m} \quad \boxed{m} \!\to\!$

The speed of each truck is v.

(b) Speed of approach $= u + v$
    $\Rightarrow$ speed of separation $= u + v$

So after collision, the trucks have speeds w and $w + u + v$.

By conservation of momentum,

$mu - mv = mw + mw + mu + mv$

$\implies \quad w = -v$

So the velocities are $-v$ and u.

(c) In (a), the total kinetic energy before the collision is

$$\tfrac{1}{2}mv^2 + \tfrac{1}{2}mv^2 = mv^2$$

Since the speed of each truck is unaltered after the collision, the total kinetic energy after the collision, is mv^2 also.

In (b), the total kinetic energy before the collision is

$$\tfrac{1}{2}mu^2 + \tfrac{1}{2}mv^2$$

The total kinetic energy after the collision is also $\tfrac{1}{2}mu^2 + \tfrac{1}{2}mv^2$.

C Newton's law of restitution (p. 16)

Exercise C (p. 18)

1 (a) 0.7

(b) $v^2 = 5g \implies v = 7 \text{ m s}^{-1}$
Speed immediately after = 4.9 m s^{-1}

$$h = \frac{4.9^2}{2g} = 1.225 \text{ m}$$

Notice that this is $e^2 \times 2.5$, or $e^2 \times$ initial height.

3 The ball hits the floor at $\sqrt{25 + 2g}$ m s^{-1}.
It leaves the floor at $\sqrt{2g}$ m s^{-1}. $e = 0.67$

4 Speed of approach $= 3 + 1 = 4$ m s^{-1},
so speed of separation $= 1$ m s^{-1}.
Final speed of first truck $= 1$ m s^{-1},
and its mass $= 3$ kg

5 $1\tfrac{1}{2}$ m s^{-1}, 3 m s^{-1}

6 (a) 2.1 m s^{-1}, 3.1 m s^{-1}; 6.3 N s; 3.15 J
(b) 0.2 m s^{-1}, 1.2 m s^{-1}; 12.6 N s; 25.2 J
(c) −0.7 m s^{-1}, 3.3 m s^{-1}; 18.9 N s; 9.45 J
(d) 2.4 m s^{-1}, 2.4 m s^{-1}; 4.2 N s; 4.2 J
(e) 0.5 m s^{-1}, 0.5 m s^{-1}; 10.5 N s; 26.25 J
(f) −3 m s^{-1}, 7 m s^{-1}; 42 N s; 0 J

7 Half of the KE

8 (a) The ball drops straight down to the base of the wall.

(b) The ball returns to the starting point.

If $e = \tfrac{2}{3}$, the ball lands $\tfrac{2}{3}$ of the way from the wall to the starting point.

9E

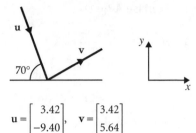

$$\mathbf{u} = \begin{bmatrix} 3.42 \\ -9.40 \end{bmatrix}, \quad \mathbf{v} = \begin{bmatrix} 3.42 \\ 5.64 \end{bmatrix}$$

$\mathbf{v}$ is 6.6 m s^{-1} at 59° to the surface.

10 $\mathbf{u} = \begin{bmatrix} a \\ b \end{bmatrix} \implies \mathbf{v}_1 = \begin{bmatrix} -ea \\ b \end{bmatrix} \implies \mathbf{v}_2 = \begin{bmatrix} -ea \\ -eb \end{bmatrix}$, taking the x-axis at right angles to the first cushion.

$\mathbf{v}_2 = -e\begin{bmatrix} a \\ b \end{bmatrix}$, which is parallel to $\mathbf{u}$.

This assumes that the ball can be treated as a particle and has no sidespin.

3 Circular motion

A Angular speed (p. 20)

1 $\dfrac{3000 \times 2\pi}{60} = 314 \text{ rad s}^{-1}$

2 The penny travels $2\pi r$ metres in $\dfrac{2\pi}{2}$ seconds, giving a speed of $2r = 0.12$ m s^{-1}.

3 The velocity is 0.12 m s^{-1} tangentially. The speed is constant but the velocity is changing all the time.

4 (a) 3 cm from the centre
(b) 12 cm from the centre

5 $\tfrac{1}{2}\pi \div 2 = 0.785$ s

6 (a) $(0.032, 0.05)$ (b) $(-0.025, 0.055)$
(c) $(-0.039, -0.045)$

7 $(0.06 \cos 2t, 0.06 \sin 2t)$

8 $\begin{bmatrix} -0.101 \\ 0.065 \end{bmatrix}, \begin{bmatrix} -1.09 \\ -0.050 \end{bmatrix}, \begin{bmatrix} 0.091 \\ -0.078 \end{bmatrix}$

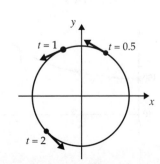

Exercise A (p. 22)

1   $50 \text{ r.p.m.} = \dfrac{50 \times 2\pi}{60} \text{ rad s}^{-1}$

Speed of tip is $\dfrac{4 \times 50 \times 2\pi}{60} \text{ m s}^{-1}$

$= 21 \text{ m s}^{-1} \text{ (to 2 s.f.)}$

2   Angular speed,

$\omega = \dfrac{v}{r} = \dfrac{1}{0.1} \text{ rad s}^{-1} = 10 \text{ rad s}^{-1}$

3   1.26 rad s^{-1}

4   $\omega = \dfrac{7\pi}{1.5} = 14.7 \text{ rad s}^{-1}$

Speed $= 10.3 \text{ m s}^{-1}$

5   Number of revolutions $= \dfrac{2.5 \times 30}{2\pi} = 11.9$

Speed $= 10 \text{ m s}^{-1}$

6   $500 \text{ rpm} = \dfrac{500 \times 2\pi}{60} \text{ rad s}^{-1} \approx 52 \text{ rad s}^{-1}$

$1000 \text{ rpm} \approx 105 \text{ rad s}^{-1}$

The speed of a point on the drum varies
between $\dfrac{500 \times 2\pi \times 0.6}{60} \text{ m s}^{-1}$ and double
this, i.e. between 31.4 and 62.8 m s^{-1}.

7   (a) $v = r\omega = \dfrac{6.37 \times 10^{6} \times 2\pi}{24 \times 60 \times 60} \text{ m s}^{-1}$

$\approx 464 \text{ m s}^{-1}$

   (b) The speed at the north pole is zero.

8E The cotton on the outside of the reel
unwinds at 3 m s^{-1}.

The angular speed is $\dfrac{3}{0.02} = 150 \text{ rad s}^{-1}$.

When the reel is nearly empty the angular
speed is $\dfrac{3}{0.01} \text{ rad s}^{-1} = 300 \text{ rad s}^{-1}$.

After 25 seconds half the cotton will have
gone, but the diameter of the reel will be
greater than 1.5 cm, so the angular speed is
less than 200 rad s^{-1}.

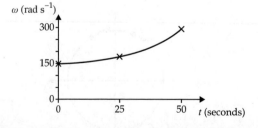

B Acceleration (p. 23)

1   $\mathbf{v} = \begin{bmatrix} -r\omega \sin \omega t \\ r\omega \cos \omega t \end{bmatrix}$

2   $\mathbf{a} = \begin{bmatrix} -r\omega^{2} \cos \omega t \\ -r\omega^{2} \sin \omega t \end{bmatrix} = -\omega^{2}\mathbf{r}$

so $a = r\omega^{2} = r\left(\dfrac{v}{r}\right)^{2} = \dfrac{v^{2}}{r}$

The direction is towards the centre of the
circle.

Exercise B (p. 25)

1   4.1 rad s^{-1}

2   19 m s^{-2}

3   $120 \text{ km h}^{-1} = \dfrac{120 \times 1000}{3600} \text{ m s}^{-1}$

The acceleration $\dfrac{v^{2}}{r} = 30 \text{ m s}^{-2}$, so the

radius is $\left(\dfrac{120}{3.6}\right)^{2} \div 30 \text{ m} \approx 37 \text{ metres}$

4   $10 \text{ rpm.} = 1.05 \text{ rad s}^{-1}$

   (a) Her speed is $1 \times 1.05 \text{ m s}^{-1} \approx 1.1 \text{ m s}^{-1}$

Her acceleration is $1 \times \left(\dfrac{\pi}{3}\right)^{2} \approx 1.1 \text{ m s}^{-2}$

   (b) Her speed is 2.1 m s^{-1} and her
acceleration is 2.2 m s^{-2} (to 2 s.f.).

At 1 metre from the centre, the force
towards the centre is 30×1.1 N or 33 N.

At 2 metres from the centre the force is
doubled to 66 N.

5   The acceleration is
$0.5^{2} \times 0.15 = 0.0375 \text{ m s}^{-2}$ towards the
centre of the circle.

$F = 0.004 \times 0.0375 = 0.000\,15 \text{ N}$

This force is towards the centre of the
turntable and is due to friction.

$\dfrac{F}{N} \leqslant \mu \quad \Longrightarrow \quad \dfrac{0.000\,15}{0.04} \leqslant \mu$

$\Longrightarrow \quad \mu \geqslant 0.003\,75$

The coefficient of friction is greater than
or equal to 0.003 75.

6 Let the block have mass m kilograms and be modelled as a particle 0.2 metres from the axis of rotation. Let the angular speed be ω rad s^{-1}.

Acceleration $= \omega^2 \times 0.2$ towards the centre, force $= 0.2m\omega^2$

In limiting friction, $F = \mu N = 0.3mg$

$0.2m\omega^2 = 0.3mg$

$\Rightarrow \quad \omega = 3.87$ rad s^{-1} (to 3 s.f.)

The turntable must spin with an angular speed of over 3.87 rad s^{-1} for the block to slide off.

7E 1 revolution in 6 seconds $= \dfrac{2\pi}{6}$ rad s^{-1}

$$= 1.05 \text{ rad s}^{-1}$$

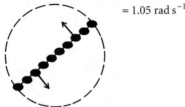

Assume that each skater is 0.8 metre from elbow to elbow. You can model the skater as a particle half-way along this 80 cm length.

Assume that the mass of each skater is 65 kg.

(a) The furthest skater makes a circle of radius 3.6 metres and the central skaters make circles of radius 0.4 metre.

The speeds of the outside skaters are therefore 3.8 m s^{-1} and those of the central skaters are 0.42 m s^{-1}.

(b) The acceleration of the outside pair is 3.96 m s^{-2} radially inwards.

(c) Now $\mathbf{F} = m\mathbf{a}$ so the force is 257 newtons to 3 s.f. (Remember this is the resultant force. What do you think the force on each arm of the central skaters will be?)

C   Gravity (p. 26)

1 $\dfrac{GE}{R^2} = g \implies E = \dfrac{gR^2}{G}$

$E \approx 6 \times 10^{24}$ kg

Knowing the mass of the Earth enabled astronomers to calculate the mass of the Sun, Moon and planets from observations of their gravitational effect on each other.

2 Weight $= \dfrac{G \times 80 \times 7.34 \times 10^{22}}{1\,738\,000^2} = 130$ N

This is about one sixth of his weight on the Earth's surface.

Exercise C (p. 29)

1 (a) Change in momentum $= 4g \times 3$

≈ 118 kg m s^{-1}

(b) Change in Earth's velocity $= \dfrac{118}{5.98 \times 10^{24}}$

$\approx 1.97 \times 10^{-23}$ m s^{-1},

which is negligible.

2 (a) (i) 9.80 N   (ii) 9.77 N   (iii) 7.47 N

(b) 2.45 N

(c) Weight

(newtons)

Distance above sea level (10^6 metres)

3 $\frac{1}{80} \div \left(\frac{3}{11}\right)^2 = \frac{121}{720}$

The acceleration due to gravity on the Moon is about $\frac{121}{720}g$, giving a weight of 99 N.

4 Weight $= 400g \times \left(\dfrac{6380}{7380}\right)^2$

$= 2900$ N

$\dfrac{mv^2}{r} = 2900 \implies v = 7400$ m s^{-1}

5 The force due to gravity $\propto \dfrac{1}{r^2}$ and it is equal to $\dfrac{mv^2}{r}$.

So $\dfrac{mv^2}{r} \propto \dfrac{1}{r^2}$,

$v^2 \propto \dfrac{1}{r}$

This means that v^2 is multiplied by

$\dfrac{6380 + 4000}{6380 + 3500} \approx 1.05$.

Hence v is multiplied by about 1.025, meaning a 2.5% increase.

6 (a) 2.7×10^{-6} rad s^{-1}

(b) 2.7×10^{-3} m s^{-2}

(c) $\dfrac{GEm}{r^2} = m \times 2.7 \times 10^{-3}$

$\Rightarrow E = \dfrac{(3.84 \times 10^8)^2 \times 2.72 \times 10^{-3}}{6.67 \times 10^{-11}}$

$\Rightarrow E = 6.0 \times 10^{24}$ kg

7 $\dfrac{GEM_S}{r^2} = Er\omega^2 \Rightarrow M_S = 2.0 \times 10^{30}$ kg

8 $\dfrac{GE}{R^2} = g$ and $\dfrac{GEm}{r^2} = mr\omega^2$

$\Rightarrow r^3\omega^2 = GE = gR^2$

9 $\omega = \dfrac{2\pi}{24 \times 3600}$

From question 8, $r^3\omega^2 = gR^2$, giving

$r = 4.2 \times 10^7$ m

$= 4.2 \times 10^4$ km

The satellite must be 3.6×10^4 km above the Earth's surface.

Speed $= r\omega = 3.1$ km s^{-1}.

10 $T = \dfrac{2\pi}{\omega}$ and $D^3\omega^2 =$ constant (from question 8).

Hence $\dfrac{T^2}{D^3}$ is constant.

4 Centres of mass

A Moments (p. 31)

Exercise A (p. 33)

1 Total moment about A
$= 50 \times 4 + 100 \times 6$
$= 800$ N m anticlockwise

2 The moment of the force **W** about O is $Wa \sin \phi$ N m clockwise.
The moment of the force **P** about O is $2Pa \cos \phi$ N m anticlockwise.

3 (a) The moment of the 10 newton force about O $= 10 \times 0.24 \times \sin 50°$
$= 1.84$ N m clockwise.
The moment of the 6 newton force about O $= 1.84$ N m anticlockwise.
The moment of the 16 newton force about O $= 16 \times 0 = 0$

(b) The moment of the 10 newton force about A $= 10 \times 0 = 0$
The moment of the 6 newton force about A $= 2.94$ N m anticlockwise.
The moment of the 16 newton force about A $= 2.94$ N m clockwise.

4 The moment of the force **T** about O $= Tl \sin \phi$ but $\sin \phi$ is a maximum when $\phi = 90°$, so the turning effect will be greatest when $\sin \phi = 1$. She should pull vertically upwards.

5 The wheel of the wheelbarrow acts as a pivot. If the wheelbarrow handles are three times as far from the wheel as the centre of the barrow part is, then Carole's lifting force is approximately 300 N.

6

The line of action of Winston's weight will be $2 \cos 30° + 2 \sin 30°$ metres from the pivot, so Winston's weight will produce a clockwise moment of

$20g(2 \cos 30° + 2 \sin 30°) = 535$ N m

Josie's weight will be $2 \cos 30° - 2 \sin 30°$ metres from the pivot and will produce an anticlockwise moment of

$60g(2 \cos 30° - 2 \sin 30°) = 430$ N m

Winston's weight has the greater turning effect.

7 (a) Assume that the plank is weightless, that they sit right at the ends of the plank, and that Josie is x metres from the pivot. The moment of Josie about the pivot is $60gx$ anticlockwise. The moment of Winston is $20g(3 - x)$ clockwise. These must balance, so

$$60gx = 60g - 20gx \implies x = 0.75$$

Josie must be 0.75 metres from the pivot.

(b) The plank would provide an extra clockwise moment and the pivot would therefore be slightly farther away from Josie than the 0.75 metres calculated in part (a).

B Centre of gravity (p. 35)

1 Taking moments about the centre point,

$$6d' = 4 \times 0.2 - 1 \times 0.2$$
$$d' = 0.1$$

Taking moments about the centre of the right-hand mass,

$$6d'' = 1 \times 0.2 + 1 \times 0.4$$
$$d'' = 0.1$$

The same position is found in each case.

Exercise B (p. 36)

1 (a) Taking moments about the centre of the 3 N weight, C, as the pivot,

$$2 \times 0.4 + 2 \times 0.8 = 7X$$

where X is the distance of the centre of gravity from C.

$$X = 0.343 \text{ metres}$$

The centre of gravity is 34.3 cm from the 3 newton weight (to 3 s.f.).

(b) Taking moments about the unweighted end of the rod,

$$0.5 \times 2 + 1 \times 3 = 5X$$
$$X = 0.8 \text{ metres}$$

The centre of gravity is 80 cm from the unweighted end of the rod. Notice that it divides the distance between the weights in the ratio 3 : 2.

2 (a) $25A = 30 + 80 + 40$
     $\implies A = 6$ N
   (b) $25B = 95 + 120 + 10$
     $\implies B = 9$ N
   (c) $C = 6$ N, $D = 9$ N

3 Moments about the right-hand support give

$$20W + 25E = 140 + 60 + 50 = 250$$

Also $E + F = 4 + 3 + 10 + W$

(a) $W = 5$ N $\implies$ $E = 6$ N, $F = 16$ N
(b) $W = 10$ N $\implies$ $E = 2$ N, $F = 25$ N
(c) $E = 0$ when the ruler lifts off the left support.
     Then $W = 12.5$ N.

4

Movement	Displacement in the direction of the		
	x-axis	y-axis	z-axis
(a)	zero	zero	positive
(b)	zero	positive	negative
(c)	positive	negative	zero
(d)	positive	zero	negative

C Centre of mass (p. 38)

1 (a) $m = 6.3$

2 The centre of gravity of the lamina lies on the mean of the histogram. It is, in effect, the mean position of the mass.

Notice that a line through the centre of gravity does not necessarily divide the area of the lamina into two equal parts.

3 $\bar{x} = \dfrac{18 \times 3 + 2 \times 1}{18 + 2} = 2.8$

   $\bar{y} = \dfrac{18 \times 1.5 + 2 \times 3.5}{18 + 2} = 1.7$

Exercise C (p. 41)

1 (a)   (b)

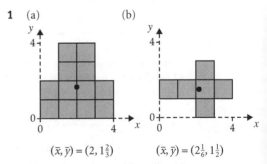

$(\bar{x}, \bar{y}) = (2, 1\tfrac{2}{3})$ $(\bar{x}, \bar{y}) = (2\tfrac{1}{6}, 1\tfrac{1}{2})$

(c)   (d)

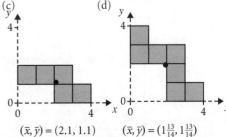

$(\bar{x}, \bar{y}) = (2.1, 1.1)$ $(\bar{x}, \bar{y}) = (1\tfrac{13}{14}, 1\tfrac{13}{14})$

(e)

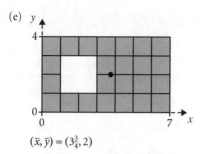

$$(\bar{x}, \bar{y}) = (3\tfrac{3}{4}, 2)$$

(f)

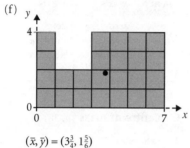

$$(\bar{x}, \bar{y}) = (3\tfrac{3}{4}, 1\tfrac{5}{6})$$

2 Assume that the centres of gravity of the spheres are at their geometric centres. The total mass of the toy is 100 grams.

Taking the axes shown, if the centre of gravity of the toy is at $(\bar{x}, \bar{y})$ and taking moments about A,

$$1 \times \bar{x} = 0.2 \times 60$$
$$\Rightarrow \bar{x} = 12$$

Similarly $\bar{y} = 20$

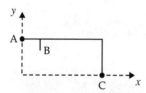

Hence the pin must be a fixed distance 12 cm along the rod from the centre of the large sphere and must be 5 cm long.

3 $\bar{x} = \dfrac{0.2 \times 0.9 + 0.1 \times 0.45}{0.3} = 0.75$

Centre of mass is 0.75 m from the end of the rod.

4 0.175 kg

5

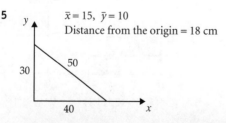

$\bar{x} = 15$, $\bar{y} = 10$
Distance from the origin = 18 cm

6 $\bar{x} = 1.5$ by symmetry in each case

$$\bar{y} = \frac{4 \times 2 + 3 \times 4.5}{7} = 3.1 \text{ for the lamina}$$

$$\bar{y} = \frac{8 \times 2 + 2 \times 4.5 + 3 \times 5 + 2 \times 4 + 1 \times 0}{16}$$

$$= 3 \text{ for the wire}$$

7E $\dfrac{150\bar{x} + 50 \times 5}{150 + 50} = 10$ or $\bar{x} = \dfrac{200 \times 10 - 50 \times 5}{200 - 50}$

$\bar{x} = 11\tfrac{2}{3}$; $\bar{y} = 5$ by symmetry

D Applications (p. 43)

1 G is always vertically below the point of suspension.

Exercise D (p. 44)

1 The centre of mass is where the medians meet. A median of a triangle joins a vertex to the mid-point of the opposite side.

2 (a) $\bar{x} = \tfrac{13}{14}$, $\bar{y} = \tfrac{27}{14}$
    The centre of mass is $\tfrac{13}{14}$ units to the right of A and $\tfrac{43}{14}$ units below A. When the lamina is suspended from A, the angle between AB and the vertical is $\tan^{-1} \tfrac{13}{43} \approx 17°$.

   (b) $\bar{x} = \tfrac{21}{18}$, $\bar{y} = \tfrac{53}{18}$
    The angle is $\tan^{-1} \tfrac{21}{37} \approx 30°$.

3 Assuming the weight is equally distributed over the box and its interior (which is not very likely), the diagram represents the situation.

From the diagram,

$a = 0.6 \cos 45°$
$b = 1.4 \cos 45°$

Taking moments about the bottom corner,

$a \times 750 = (a + b)P$
$\Rightarrow \quad P = 225$ newtons

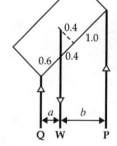

Resolving vertically,

$P + Q = 750$
$\Rightarrow \quad Q = 525$ newtons

The stronger man needs to be at the bottom. (However, the top position is more difficult and uncomfortable in practice.)

Each hand should provide half the required lift, so the supporting force provided by each hand is 262.5 newtons from the man at the bottom and 112.5 newtons from the man at the top.

4 (a)

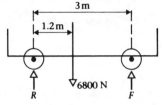

Assume the load on each of the front wheels is the same.

Assume that the load on each of the rear wheels is the same.

Assume that the contact force between the wheels and the road is normal to the road surface.

Taking moments about the rear axle,

$$3 \times F = 1.2 \times 6800$$
$$\Rightarrow \qquad F = 2720 \text{ newtons}$$
$$R + F = 6800 \text{ newtons}$$
$$\text{so} \qquad R = 4080 \text{ newtons}$$

The total reaction at each front wheel is 1360 newtons.

The total reaction at each rear wheel is 2040 newtons.

(b) Each rear wheel carries 2220 N and each front wheel carries 1480 N.

(c) With the luggage in the boot the forces acting are as shown.

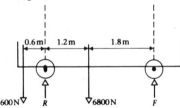

Considering moments about the front axle,

$$R \times 3 = 600 \times 3.6 + 6800 \times 1.8$$
$$\Rightarrow \qquad R = 4800 \text{ newtons}$$

Considering moments about the rear axle,

$$F \times 3 + 600 \times 0.6 = 6800 \times 1.2$$
$$\Rightarrow \qquad F = 2600 \text{ newtons}$$

Each rear wheel will carry 2400 newtons.
Each front wheel will carry 1300 newtons.

5

With the notation in the figure, taking moments about J,

$$T \times 0.02 = 27 \times 0.13 + W \times 0.3$$

(a) When $W = 0$, $T = 175.5$
The tension is about 180 newtons.
(b) When $W = 45$, $T = 850.5$
The tension is about 850 newtons.

This is, of course, a very greatly simplified model of the real situation.

6 Because the box does not slip,

$$P \leqslant \tfrac{1}{3} \times 24 = 8 \text{ N}$$

Because the box does not tip,

$$20P \leqslant 24 \times 5$$
$$P \leqslant 6 \text{ N}$$

So P must be less than 6 newtons.

7 $\bar{x} = \dfrac{h + r}{2}$

(a) $h = 2r \implies \bar{x} = 1\tfrac{1}{2}r < h$
(b) $h = \tfrac{1}{2}r \implies \bar{x} = \tfrac{3}{4}r > h$
(c) $h = r \implies \bar{x} = r = h$

In (a), the body will not move. In (b), it will rotate and settle down with its axis vertical. In (c), the body could theoretically rest with any point of the hemispherical surface in contact with the table.

5 Variable forces in one dimension

A **Impulse** (p. 47)

1D Impulse = change in momentum
$$= 0.1 \times 5 - 0.1 \times (-9)$$
$$= 1.4 \text{ N s}$$

$Ft = 1.4 \implies F = 140 \text{ N}$

2 Impulse on 5 kg body = 15 N s to the left

Average force = 2500 N

Impulse on 3 kg body = 15 N s to the right
$v = 5 \text{ m s}^{-1}$

3 $\begin{bmatrix} -2 \\ 1 \end{bmatrix}$ N s

4 $I = 0.15 \begin{bmatrix} -7.5 \\ 13.0 \end{bmatrix} - 0.15 \begin{bmatrix} 10 \\ 0 \end{bmatrix} = \begin{bmatrix} -2.62 \\ 1.95 \end{bmatrix}$

This is 3.3 N s at 143° to the initial direction.

Average force = $\begin{bmatrix} -525 \\ 390 \end{bmatrix}$ N

5 $\displaystyle\int_0^a (t^3 - 2at^2 + a^2 t)\, dt$

$= \left[\tfrac{1}{4}t^4 - \tfrac{2}{3}at^3 + \tfrac{1}{2}a^2 t^2 \right]_0^a$

$= \tfrac{1}{12}a^4$

$= 2.13 \times 10^{-11}$ when $a = 0.004$

Exercise A (p. 50)

1   (a) 4.5 N s   (b) 7.5 N s

2   The change in momentum is

$\dfrac{90}{1000} \times 8 + \dfrac{90}{1000} \times 6 = 1.26$ N s

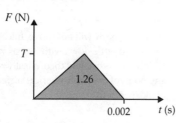

F (N)

T

1.26

0.002 t (s)

The maximum force T satisfies

$T \times 0.001 = 1.26$

$\Rightarrow$ $T = 1260$ newtons

3   Using the trapezium rule, the total impulse is approximately

$10 \times (850 + 565 + 370 + 215 + 150 + 105)$
$= 22\,550$ N s

The final speed is therefore approximately 23 m s^{-1}.

4   (a) $\tfrac{1}{2} \times 160 \times 0.08 = 6.4$ N s

(b) $10^5 \left[0.04t^2 - \tfrac{1}{3}t^3 \right]_0^{0.08} = 8.5$ N s

5   (a) Impulse = $\left[40 \ln(t + 0.1) - 200t \right]_0^{0.1}$

$= 7.73$ N s
Speed = 26 m s^{-1}

(b) Impulse = $\left[200t + \dfrac{40}{\pi} \cos 5\pi t \right]_0^{0.1}$

$= 7.27$ N s
Speed = 24 m s^{-1}

(c) Impulse = $\left[-\dfrac{250}{k} e^{-kt} - 50t \right]_0^{0.1}$

$= 7.43$ N s
Speed = 25 m s^{-1}

6

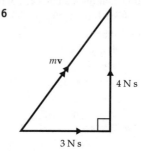

mv

4 N s

3 N s

Final velocity is 33 m s^{-1} at 53° to the original direction, i.e. past the gully fieldsman.

B   Work done by a variable force
(p. 51)

1   Assume, as a reasonable approximation, that the force is 3800 N during the first 10 metres, 3675 N during the next 10 metres, and so on. The work done in each 10-metre interval is then as follows.

Distance travelled (m)	0–10	10–20	20–30	30–40	40–50
Work done (J)	38 000	36 750	35 000	32 750	30 000
Total work done (J)	38 000	74 750	109 750	142 500	172 500

The total kinetic energy equals the total work done and is 38 000 joules in the first 10 metres.

$38\,000 = \tfrac{1}{2} \times 1000 \times v^2 - \tfrac{1}{2} \times 1000 \times 0^2$

$\Rightarrow$ $v^2 = 76$

The speed is approximately 8.7 m s^{-1}. Similarly, the speeds after 20, 30, 40 and 50 metres are 12.2, 14.8, 16.9 and 18.6 m s^{-1}. The total kinetic energy has been obtained by adding the areas under the step graph.

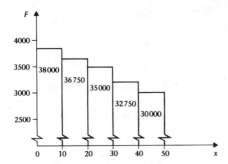

2 You might expect a better approximation to be obtained by drawing a continuous curve through the known points and finding the area under the graph.

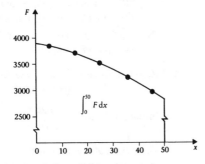

The general result is

$$\int F \, dx = \tfrac{1}{2}mv^2 - \tfrac{1}{2}mu^2$$

Exercise B (p. 53)

1

Distance (m)	0	1	2	3	4
Force (N)	400	300	240	210	190
Average force over interval (N)		350	270	225	200
Kinetic energy* (J)		350	620	845	1045
Velocity (m s^{-1})		8.4	11.1	13.0	14.5

Distance (m)	4	5	6	7	8
Force (N)	190	160	130	80	0
Average force over interval (N)		175	145	105	40
Kinetic energy* (J)	1045	1220	1365	1470	1510
Velocity (m s^{-1})	14.5	15.6	16.5	17.1	17.4

* For instance, the energy after 2 m is $(350 \times 1 + 270 \times 1)$ joules

2 (a) $\text{WD} = \left[\tfrac{5}{2}x^2\right]_0^6 = 90$ J

(b) $\text{WD} = \left[30x - \tfrac{3}{2}x^2\right]_0^2 = 54$ J

(c) $\text{WD} = \left[-\dfrac{120}{x}\right]_2^8 = 45$ J

(d) $\text{WD} = \left[-\tfrac{9}{2}x^2\right]_5^1 = 108$ J

3 Kinetic energy acquired

$$= \int_0^{50} (4000 - 22.5x - 0.25x^2) \, dx$$

$$= \left[4000x - \frac{22.5x^2}{2} - \frac{0.25x^3}{3}\right]_0^{50}$$

$$= 161\,500 \text{ J}$$

Speed, v m s^{-1}, is given by

$$161\,500 = \tfrac{1}{2} \times 1400 \times v^2$$

$$\implies \qquad v = 15.2$$

After 50 metres, the van is travelling at 15 m s^{-1} (about 55 km h^{-1}).

4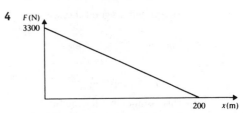

The (distance, force) graph is as shown. The kinetic energy acquired equals the area under this graph over the appropriate interval.

By inspection.

$$F = 3300 - \frac{3300x}{200} = 3300 - 16.5x$$

The kinetic energy (J) acquired during the first x metres is

$$\int_0^x (3300 - 16.5x) \, dx = 3300x - 8.25x^2$$

Distance (m)	0	50	100	150	200
Kinetic energy (J)	0	144 400	247 500	309 400	330 000
Speed (m s^{-1})	0	17.0*	22.2	24.9	25.7

* $144\,400 = \tfrac{1}{2} \times 1000 \times v^2$ gives $v = 17.0$

The shape of the (distance, speed) graph is as illustrated.

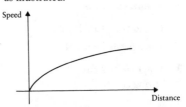

5 $\left[4000x - \frac{1}{2}kx^2\right]_0^{0.6} = \frac{1}{2} \times 0.015 \times 500^2$

$\Rightarrow \qquad 0.18k = 2400 - 1875$

$\Rightarrow \qquad\qquad k = 2900$

6 $WD = \left[-\dfrac{mgR^2}{x}\right]_{6.4 \times 10^6}^{6.6 \times 10^6}$

$\qquad = 1.9 \times 10^9 \text{ J}$

7 $\left[-\dfrac{mgR^2}{x}\right]_R^{R+h} = \frac{1}{2}mu^2$

$\Rightarrow \qquad R + h = 6436 \text{ km}$

The projectile rises about 36 km.

If weight change is ignored,

$\qquad mgh = \frac{1}{2}mu^2$

$\qquad\quad h = 35 \text{ km}$

This provides a good check.

8 $\frac{1}{2}mu^2 > \left[-\dfrac{mgR^2}{x}\right]_R^{\infty} = mgR$

$\qquad u > 1.1 \times 10^4 \text{ m s}^{-1}$

This assumes that the motors cut out reasonably close to the Earth's surface but that air resistance can be ignored.

9 (a) 2.54×10^8 J

(b) 4.1×10^3 m s^{-1}

(c) Air resistance slows meteorites down. The energy is converted into heat so that meteorites are quite hot when they land.

C Springs and elastic strings (p. 55)

1 If the weights are not too large, you should find that extension is roughly proportional to weight.

2 Yes, confirming what was found in question 1.

Exercise C (p. 56)

1 3 cm, 4 cm, $\frac{1}{2}$ cm

2 (a) 40 cm   (b) $27\frac{1}{2}$ cm

Force needed = 6.4 N

3 Length = 21.2 cm
Spring constant = 2500 N m^{-1}

4 (a) 2.0033 m   (b) 50.2 m s^{-2}

5 6.9 m s^{-2}

D Elastic potential energy (p. 57)

Exercise D (p. 58)

1 (a) 0.125 J   (b) 1.125 J

2 40 N m^{-1}

3 (a) 0.625 J   (b) $2.5 - 0.625 = 1.875$ J

4 (a) Length $= 2\sqrt{16^2 + 8^2} = 35.8$ cm
Extension = 0.158 m
EPE $= \frac{1}{2} \times 600 \times 0.158^2 = 7.49$ J
Tension $= T = 600 \times 0.158 = 94.6$ N

(b) $\frac{1}{2}mv^2 = 7.49 \Rightarrow v = 19.4$
The speed is 19 m s^{-1}

5E Resultant force $= 2T\cos\theta$ where $\tan\theta = \frac{8}{16}$
$\qquad\qquad\qquad = 169$ N $= 170$ N (to 2 s.f.)

Initial acceleration $= \dfrac{169}{0.04} = 4200$ m s^{-2}
$\qquad\qquad\qquad\qquad\qquad$ (to 2 s.f.)

The weight of the stone affects the answer by a small amount which depends on the direction in which the stone is catapulted.

6 (a) We assume that mechanical energy is conserved.

KE gained $= \frac{1}{2}mv^2$
$\qquad\qquad = \frac{1}{28}g \times 0.02 - \frac{1}{2} \times 250 \times 0.02^2$
$\Rightarrow \qquad v = 0.44$ m s^{-1}

(b) 0.37 m s^{-1}

(c) At the lowest point, KE = 0.
$\frac{1}{2} \times 250 \times x^2 = \frac{1}{2} \times g \times x \Rightarrow x = 0.039$
The greatest extension of the spring is 3.9 cm.

6 Modelling circular motion

A Motion in a horizontal circle (p. 60)

1 (a) Weight, normal contact force, friction
$a = r\omega^2 = 1.92$ m s^{-2}

(b) $\mu = \dfrac{F}{N} = \dfrac{1.92m}{mg} = 0.20$

(c) $\mu = \dfrac{m \times 0.2\omega^2}{mg} \Rightarrow \omega = 3.1$ rad s^{-1}

2 (a) $r = l \sin\theta$

$\left.\begin{array}{l} T\cos\theta = mg \\ T\sin\theta = mr\omega^2 \end{array}\right\} \implies \omega^2 = \dfrac{g}{l\cos\theta}$

(b) $\cos\theta = \dfrac{g}{l\omega^2} \implies \theta = 47°$

(c) As ω increases, $\cos\theta$ decreases and so θ increases. This is what you would expect.

(d) No matter how much you increase ω or l, the expression $\dfrac{g}{l\omega^2}$ is always positive; it can never reach zero. It follows that θ can only get very close to $90°$ and can never reach (or go beyond) $90°$.

(e) As l increases, θ increases.

3 (a) $\cos\theta = \dfrac{g}{l\omega^2}$ is independent of m. The heavier bob will swing out at the same angle as the lighter bob.

(b) For any length of string, l, the bob moves in a horizontal circle at a depth $l\cos\theta$ below the point of suspension, where $l\cos\theta = \dfrac{g}{\omega^2}$ is dependent only on the angular speed of the pendulum.

4 In question 2(a),

$T\sin\theta = mr\omega^2 = ml\sin\theta\omega^2$ (1)

For a conical pendulum, $T = ml\omega^2$. There is a second solution to equation (1), namely that $\sin\theta = 0$.

If $\omega < \sqrt{\dfrac{g}{l}}$, then $\sin\theta = 0$ and the string is vertical, and we are no longer dealing with the motion of a conical pendulum.

Notice that the angular speed at which a bob starts to swing out is inversely proportional to $\sqrt{l}$. When you tie two bobs to the same spindle with different lengths of string, you will find that the bob on the long string will swing out before the bob on the short string, as the angular speed increases from zero.

5 The main difference is that the 'bob' on a chair-o-plane is suspended some distance from the axis of rotation. An analysis of the chair-o-plane will have to take this into account.

Exercise A (p. 62)

1 $F = \dfrac{mv^2}{r} = 1500\text{ N}$

2 $\mu N = F = W$

$\implies \frac{2}{5} \times m \times 5 \times \omega^2 = mg$

$\implies \omega = 2.2\text{ rad s}^{-1}$

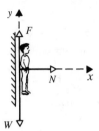

3 $\sin\theta = \dfrac{0.3}{0.8} \implies \theta = 22.0°$

$T\cos\theta = mg \implies T = 5.3\text{ N}$

$T\sin\theta = mr\omega^2 \implies \omega = 3.6\text{ rad s}^{-1}$

$\implies v = 1.1\text{ m s}^{-1}$

4 $60\cos\theta = 4g \implies \theta = 49.2°$

$\omega^2 = \dfrac{g}{l\cos\theta} \implies \omega = 3.9\text{ rad s}^{-1}$

5 $\left.\begin{array}{l} N\sin 60° = mg \\ N\cos 60° = m \times 10\omega^2 \end{array}\right\}$

$\implies \omega = 0.75\text{ rad s}^{-1}$

$\implies v = 7.5\text{ m s}^{-1}$

6 $\left.\begin{array}{l} N\cos\theta = mg \\ N\sin\theta = \dfrac{mv^2}{r} \end{array}\right\} \implies \tan\theta = \dfrac{v^2}{rg}$

$\implies \theta = 26°$

Angle of banking $= 26°$

7 6.3 m s^{-1}.

The mass is irrelevant.

8 $\omega = 140 \times \dfrac{2\pi}{60} = 14.7\text{ rad s}^{-1}$.

As in a conical pendulum,

$\cos\theta = \dfrac{g}{0.2\omega^2} \implies \theta = 77°$

Depth $= 0.2\cos\theta = 0.046\text{ m} = 4.6\text{ cm}$

9 $v = 15\text{ m s}^{-1}$

$r = \dfrac{v^2}{g\tan 20°} = 63\text{ m}$

10E $\tan \theta = \dfrac{v^2}{rg}$, as in question 6.

$\theta = 29°$

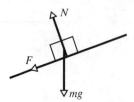

Components along the slope give

$$F + mg \sin 20° = \frac{mv^2}{r} \cos 20°$$

$$F = 2300 \text{ N}$$

11 $\dfrac{mv^2}{r} = \dfrac{mgR^2}{r^2} \implies v = 7600 \text{ m s}^{-1}$

$T = \dfrac{2\pi r}{v} = 5800 \text{ s} = 97 \text{ minutes}$

12   (a) $mr\omega^2 = T = kx \implies \omega = 8.0 \text{ rad s}^{-1}$

(b) $m(2 + x)\omega^2 = kx \implies x = 0.16$
Total length is 2.16 m.

13E $m(l + x) \sin \theta \, \omega^2 = T \sin \theta = kx \sin \theta$
$\implies x = 0.11$
The string has length 0.61 m.
$kx \cos \theta = mg \implies \theta = 63.5°$

B   **Motion in a vertical circle** (p. 64)

1D $\frac{1}{2}mv^2 = mgr \implies v = 2.4 \text{ m s}^{-1}$
N is greater than W.

2 $N - W = \dfrac{mv^2}{r} = 2mg = 2W \implies N = 3W$

Exercise B (p. 65)

1   Top: 0, 360 N; bottom: 0, 1110 N;
half-way up and down: 375 N towards
centre, 735 N

2   (a) 6.2 m s^{-1}
(b) $mgh = \frac{1}{2}m \times 3^2 \implies h = 0.46$
Maximum height above
ground = 2.46 m
(c) $T - mg = \dfrac{mv^2}{r} \implies T = 1050 \text{ N}$

3   (a) $\frac{1}{2}mv^2 - \frac{1}{2}m \times 3^2 = mg \times 0.5 \cos 60°$
$\implies$
$v = 3.7 \text{ m s}^{-1}$
(b) $T - mg \cos 60° = \dfrac{mv^2}{r} \implies T = 0.33 \text{ N}$

4   (a) $mg - \dfrac{mv^2}{r} = 1700 \text{ N}$
(b) 960 N
Greatest speed $= \sqrt{gr} = 14 \text{ m s}^{-1}$

5 $v^2 = 2g, 4g, 6g$
$T = 9800 \text{ N}, 12\,700 \text{ N}, 15\,700 \text{ N}$
If it reaches the bottom point, the tension
there will equal
$$1000g + \frac{1000 \times 10g}{10} = 19\,600 \text{ N}.$$
This is just less than the breaking strain,
which is risky.

6 $\frac{1}{2}mv^2 = mg\,(4 \cos 45° - 2)$
$\implies v = 4.0 \text{ m s}^{-1}$

7 $v = 0.89 \text{ m s}^{-1}, N = 0.0078 \text{ N}$,
$v^2 = 0.4g\,(1 - \cos \theta)$,
$N = 0.002g(3 \cos \theta - 2)$
The marble leaves the bowl when $N = 0$,
i.e. $\cos \theta = \frac{2}{3}, \theta = 48°$.

8 $v^2 = 1 + 0.4g\,(1 - \cos \theta)$
$N = mg\,(3 \cos \theta - 2) - 5m$
$N = 0$ when $3 \cos \theta = 2 + \dfrac{5}{g}$
$\theta = 33°$

9   (a) Thrust 665 N, tension 3450 N
(b) Thrust 600 N, tension 3500 N

Arms just in tension at the top
$\implies \omega = 2.9 \text{ rad s}^{-1}$.
Then the tension at the bottom = 4100 N.

10   (a) $u \leqslant \sqrt{2gl}$
The bob swings like a pendulum.
(b) $T \geqslant 0$ when $\theta = 180°$ and $\cos \theta = -1$.
$\implies u \geqslant \sqrt{5gl}$
(c)

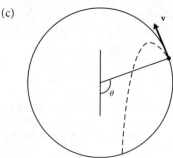

$u^2 = 3gl$
$\implies T = 0$ when $\cos \theta = -\frac{1}{3}$ and $v = \sqrt{\frac{1}{3}gl}$
The bob then moves under gravity
until the string becomes taut again.

7 Energy transfer

A Elastic potential energy (p. 68)

1D (a) $EPE = \frac{1}{2} \times 600 \times 0.15^2 = 6.75$ J

(b) $\frac{1}{2}mv^2 = 6.75 \implies v = 16.4$ m s^{-1}

(c) $mgh = 6.75 \implies h = 13.8$ m

(d) $\frac{1}{2}mv^2 = 6.75 - mg \times 6$
$\implies v = 12.3$ m s^{-1}

Exercise A (p. 71)

1 Let the tension in the string, T newtons, be given by $T = kx$, where x metres is the extension.

$$4 = k \times 0.5 \implies k = 8$$

KE at B $= 0$
EPE at B $= \frac{1}{2} \times 8 \times 0.5^2$
PE $= 0$
KE at O $= \frac{1}{2}mv^2$
EPE at O $= 0$ (string is unstretched)
PE $= 0$

Total mechanical energy is conserved

$\implies \quad 0 + 1 + 0 = 0.025v^2 + 0 + 0$
$\implies \qquad\qquad v^2 = 40$
$\qquad\qquad\qquad v = 6.32$ m s^{-1}

The speed of the mass as it passes O is 6.32 m s^{-1}.

2 Extension = final length − original length
$\qquad\qquad\quad = -0.04$ metre
(negative because the spring is compressed)
EPE stored in spring when compressed
$$= \frac{kx^2}{2} = 0.8 \text{ J}$$

The energy of the system is conserved.
Initial (PE + EPE + KE)
$\qquad\qquad = $ Final (PE + EPE + KE)
$\qquad 0 + 0.8 + 0 = PE + 0 + 0$
$\qquad PE = mgh = 0.8$

$\implies \qquad h = \dfrac{0.8}{0.02 \times 9.8} = 4.1$ m

Estimated height = 4.1 metres

NB: KE is zero initially at ground level and zero momentarily at the maximum height reached.

3 (a) Let the spring constant be k.
$0.1 \times g = k \times 0.1$
$\implies k = 9.8$ N m^{-1}
Let the gravitational potential energy be measured relative to O, the point where the top of the spring is attached.

$KE = \frac{1}{2}mv^2$
$PE = -mg(0.2 + x) = -0.98(0.2 + x)$
$EPE = \dfrac{10 \times x^2}{2}$

At the point of release:

$KE = 0$, PE $= -0.39$, EPE $= \dfrac{10 \times 0.2^2}{2}$

When the spring is 0.3 m long:

$KE = \frac{1}{2}mv^2$, PE $= -0.29$, EPE $= \dfrac{10 \times 0.1^2}{2}$

But total mechanical energy is conserved.
$0 - 0.39 + 0.2 = 0.05v^2 - 0.29 + 0.05$
$\implies \quad 0.05v^2 = 0.05$
$\qquad\qquad v = 1$ m s^{-1}

(b) Its elastic potential energy is greatest at the point of release.

4 (a) $T = kx \implies 20 = 500x$
Its extension is 0.04 metre.

(b) Let the unstretched position be O.
Initial PE $= -2 \times 9.8 \times 0.1$
Initial KE $= 0$
Initial EPE $= \frac{1}{2} \times 500 \times 0.1^2$
Final PE $= 0$
Final KE $= \frac{1}{2} \times 2 \times v^2$
Final EPE $= 0$

Total mechanical energy is conserved, so
$-2.0 + 0 + 2.5 = 0 + v^2 + 0$
$\qquad\qquad v^2 = 0.5$
$\qquad\qquad v = 0.71$ m s^{-1}

5 (a) PE lost by stunt actor $= 78 \times 9.8 \times 200$
$\qquad\qquad\qquad\qquad\qquad = 153\,000$ J

Extension of rope
$\quad = $ height − unstretched length
$\quad = 200 - 100 = 100$ m

Spring constant, $k = 30$ N m^{-1}

EPE gained by rope $= \dfrac{kx^2}{2}$

$\qquad\qquad\qquad = \dfrac{30 \times 100^2}{2}$

$\qquad\qquad\qquad = 150\,000$ J

(b) The energy of the 'system' is conserved.

Initial (PE + EPE + KE)
= Final (PE + EPE + KE)

$\rightarrow$ 153 000 + 0 + 0 = 0 + 150 000 + KE

$\Rightarrow$ Final KE = 3000 J

$$\tfrac{1}{2}mv^2 = 3000$$

$\Rightarrow$ $$v^2 = \frac{2 \times 3000}{78}$$

$\Rightarrow$ $$v = 8.8 \text{ m s}^{-1}$$

(See note (iii).)

Notes

(i) This speed is 'estimated' since the energy conservation equation which was used only dealt with mechanical energy. No account was taken of the energy lost as heat because of friction with the air and internal friction in the rope. This would reduce the KE remaining, and the final speed slightly.

(ii) The zero level for gravitational PE has been taken as ground level.

(iii) You may like to consider whether a speed of 8.8 m s^{-1} is likely to cause injury. From what height of wall would you have to jump to reach the ground at that speed?

6 $10g \times 0.2 = \tfrac{1}{2}mv^2 + \tfrac{1}{2} \times 400 \times 0.2^2$

$\Rightarrow$ $v = 1.52 \text{ m s}^{-1}$

$\tfrac{1}{2} \times 400 \times x^2 = 10gx$ $\Rightarrow$ $x = 0.49$

It comes to rest 0.49 m below the starting point.

7 In equilibrium $k \times 0.04 = 0.6g$.
Hence $k = 150 \text{ N m}^{-1}$.

PE lost + KE lost = EPE gained

$0.6g\left(\dfrac{x}{100} - 0.04\right) + \tfrac{1}{2} \times 0.6 \times 0.5^2$

$= \tfrac{1}{2} \times 150\left(\left(\dfrac{x}{100}\right)^2 - \left(\dfrac{4}{100}\right)^2\right)$

$\Rightarrow$ $x^2 - 8x + 6 = 0$

$\Rightarrow$ $x = 7.2$ or 0.8

The greatest extension is 7.2 cm. The bob will then spring back and next come to rest when the extension is 0.8 cm.

8 $70g(35 + x) = \tfrac{1}{2} \times 1000x^2$

$\Rightarrow$ $x = 7.65$

The negative root of the quadratic equation has no meaning in this situation.

9 (a) $\tfrac{1}{2} \times 70v^2 = 70g \times 37 - \tfrac{1}{2} \times 580 \times 9^2$

$\Rightarrow$ $v = 7.35 \text{ m s}^{-1}$

(b) $T = 580 \times 9 = 5220 \text{ N}$

$a = \dfrac{70g - T}{70} = -65 \text{ m s}^{-2}$

With this deceleration, the jumper will come to rest very soon after this instant.

(c) After descending 38 m, the speed is given by

$\tfrac{1}{2} \times 80v^2 = 80g \times 38 - \tfrac{1}{2} \times 580 \times 10^2$

$v = 4.4$

He is still falling after dropping 38 m.

(d) Treating a jumper as a particle is wrong. If he starts by standing on the bridge, his centre of mass is above the point of suspension. He will end up with his centre of mass below his feet and he would like his head to be well clear of the river. A substantial safety margin is advisable to cope with deficiencies in the mathematical model.

B Work and energy (p. 72)

Exercise B (p. 73)

1 $\tfrac{1}{2}k \times 1.5^2 + \tfrac{1}{2} \times 7 \times (4^2 - 2^2) = \tfrac{1}{2} \times 7g \times 3$

$\Rightarrow$ $k = 54 \text{ N m}^{-1}$

2 $\tfrac{1}{2} \times 240v^2 = (150 - 45) \times 56$

$\Rightarrow$ $v = 7 \text{ m s}^{-1}$

3 A to B:
WD by F
$= \tfrac{1}{2} \times 0.3 \times 3.5^2 - 0.3g \times 1.2 \sin 20° = 0.63 \text{ J}$

On the way down, the normal reaction and the friction force have the same magnitude as before, so the work done by friction is the same.

B to A: $\tfrac{1}{2} \times 0.3v^2 = 0.3g \times 1.2 \sin 20° - 0.631$

$v = 2.0 \text{ m s}^{-1}$

4 Total work done by friction $= \tfrac{1}{2} \times 2 \times (6^2 - 4^2)$
$= 20 \text{ J}$

WD by F on the way up = 10 J

Going up: $2g \times x \sin 15° = \tfrac{1}{2} \times 2 \times 6^2 - 10$

$x = 5.1 \text{ m}$

The total distance travelled is 10.2 m .

5 $\tfrac{1}{2} \times 0.3v^2 = 0.3g(4 \sin 30° + 6) - 1 \times 4$

$v = 11.4 \text{ m s}^{-1}$

6 $AB = \sqrt{2^2 + 1.5^2} = 2.5$ m

$\frac{1}{2} \times 0.02v^2 = 1 \times 1.5 - \frac{1}{2} \times 6 \times (2.5 - 2)^2$

$\qquad v = 8.7$ m s^{-1}

$T = 6 \times 0.5 = 3$ N

$F = ma$ gives $1 - 3 \times \dfrac{1.5}{2.5} = 0.02a$

$\qquad\qquad a = -40$ m s^{-2}

Initial acceleration is given by $1 = 0.02a$.

$a = 50$ m s^{-2}

7 Initially the strings are just unstretched since $8^2 + 15^2 = 17^2$.

When RB = 20 cm, PB = BQ $= \sqrt{15^2 + 20^2}$

$\qquad\qquad\qquad\qquad = 25$ cm

PE lost $= 0.64 \times (0.2 - 0.08) = 0.0768$ J

EPE gained $= 2 \times \frac{1}{2} \times 12 \times 0.08^2 = 0.0768$ J

The bob comes to rest when RB = 20 cm.

When RB = 14 cm,

PB = BQ $= \sqrt{15^2 + 14^2} \div 100$ m

$T = 12(\text{PB} - 0.17)$

Net force downwards $= 0.64 - 2T \times \dfrac{14}{\text{PB}}$

$\qquad\qquad\qquad = 0.064$ N > 0

So the bob is speeding up.

8 (a) Total energy provided

$= \frac{1}{2} \times 0.1 \times 1.6^2 + 0.1g \times 2 \sin 20°$

$+ 0.03 \times 6 = 0.98$ J

(b) $\frac{1}{2} \times 0.1v^2 = 0.98 - 0.03 \times 6$

$\qquad v = 4.0$ m s^{-1}

9 $F \times 10 = 1g \times 10 \sin 25° - \frac{1}{2} \times 1 \times (3^2 - 2^2)$

$F = 3.9$ N

Normal contact force $= N = 1g \cos 25°$

$\mu = \dfrac{F}{N} = 0.44$

10 (a) Friction force $= F = 0.6 \times 1.4g \cos 25°$

$\frac{1}{2} \times 1.4v^2 = \frac{1}{2} \times 1.4 \times 5^2 - F \times 10$

$\qquad\qquad\qquad + 1.4g \times 10 \sin 25°$

$\qquad v = 1.12$ m s^{-1}

(b) At impact, speed of first parcel is given by

$\frac{1}{2} \times 1.4v^2 = \frac{1}{2} \times 1.4 \times 5^2 - F \times 5$

$\qquad\qquad\qquad + 1.4g \times 5 \sin 25°$

$\qquad v = 3.62$ m s^{-1}

Speed after impact $= 1.81$ m s^{-1} since momentum is conserved.

$\frac{1}{2} \times 2.8 \times 1.81^2 + 2.8g \times x \sin 25° = 2F \times x$

$\Rightarrow \quad x = 1.38$ m

11 After 100 m, the propulsive force

$= \frac{1}{2}(4000 + 700) = 2350$ N

(a) $\frac{1}{2} \times 1000v_1^2$

$= \frac{1}{2}(4000 + 2350) \times 100 - 700 \times 100$

$v_1 = 22.2$ m s^{-1}

(b) $\frac{1}{2} \times 1000v_2^2$

$= \frac{1}{2}(4000 + 700) \times 200 - 700 \times 200$

$v_2 = 25.7$ m s^{-1}

C Power (p. 75)

Exercise C (p. 76)

1 Gain in KE $= \frac{1}{2} \times 1100 \times (35^2 - 15^2)$ J

$= 550$ kJ

Power $= \dfrac{550}{9.3} = 59$ kW

2 PE gained per second $= 25g \times 2$

$= 490$ W

KE gained per second $= \frac{1}{2} \times 25 \times 3^2$

$= 112.5$ W

Power delivered $= 490 + 112.5 = 602.5$ W

Power of pump $= 602.5 \div 0.8$

$= 750$ W (to 2 s.f.)

3 Total mass $= 25 \times 10 \times \frac{1}{2}(1 + 2.4) \times 1000$

$= 425\,000$ kg

PE gained $= 425\,000g \times 20$ J

Power delivered $= (\text{PE gained}) \div (8 \times 3600)$

Minimum power of pump $= 4.1$ kW

Some KE will also be created (c.f. question 2) but this will be small compared with the PE on this occasion. There will also be substantial friction in 20 m of pipe.

4 Useful power $= 2g \times 1.5 \div 15 = 2.0$ W

The man must work at a somewhat higher rate, because of friction.

5 (a) Net force $= \dfrac{60 \times 10^3}{30} - 1400 = 600$ N

Acceleration $= \dfrac{600}{1200} = 0.5$ m s^{-2}

(b) Total force down the slope

$= 1400 + \dfrac{1200g}{20}$

$= 1988$ N

Maximum speed $= \dfrac{60 \times 10^3}{1988}$

≈ 30 m s^{-1} (to 2 s.f.)

(c) Power $= 1988 \times 20$ W

≈ 40 kW (to 2 s.f.)

6 (a) $R = \dfrac{2000}{6} - \dfrac{90g}{15} = 270$ N

   (b) New driving force $= F = R - \dfrac{90g}{15}$

   Maximum speed $= \dfrac{1500}{F} = 7.0$ m s^{-1}

7 (a) $P = 140 \times 40 = 5600$ kW

   (b) Driving force $= F = \left(\dfrac{450g}{120} + 140\right)$ kN

   Maximum speed $= \dfrac{P}{F} = 32$ m s^{-1}

8 (a) Useful power $= 7.5g \times 2 = 150$ kW

   The power at the drum must be greater.

   (b) Force in cable $= \dfrac{240 \times 0.7}{2} = 84$ kN

   $a = \dfrac{84 - 7.5g}{7.5} = 1.4$ m s^{-2}

   (c) $v = \dfrac{240 \times 0.7}{7.5g} = 2.3$ m s^{-1}

9E (a) $\dfrac{d}{dt}(Fx) = F\dfrac{dx}{dt} = Fv$

   (b) $\dfrac{d}{dt}(\tfrac{1}{2}mv^2) = \tfrac{1}{2}m \times \dfrac{d}{dt}(v^2)$

   $= \tfrac{1}{2}m \times 2v\dfrac{dv}{dt}$ by the chain rule

   $= mva = Fv$

   (c) WD $= \displaystyle\int F\,dx \implies \dfrac{d}{dx}(\text{WD}) = F$

   $\implies \dfrac{d}{dx}(\text{WD}) \times \dfrac{dx}{dt} = Fv$

   $\implies \dfrac{d}{dt}(\text{WD}) = Fv$ by the chain rule

8 Impulse and work in two dimensions

A Constant forces (p. 78)

Exercise A (p. 81)

1 (a) 20 m s^{-1} in the opposite direction to **u**

   (b) $\mathbf{v} = 0$

   (c) 20 m s^{-1} at 60° to **v**

   (d) $m\mathbf{v} = \begin{bmatrix} 3 \\ 0 \end{bmatrix} + \begin{bmatrix} -4.70 \\ 1.71 \end{bmatrix} = \begin{bmatrix} -1.70 \\ 1.71 \end{bmatrix}$

   $= 2.41$ N s at 135° to **u**

   $\mathbf{v} = 16.1$ m s^{-1} at 135° to **u**

2 $I = \begin{bmatrix} 2.41 \\ 2.87 \end{bmatrix} - \begin{bmatrix} 4.5 \\ 0 \end{bmatrix} = \begin{bmatrix} -2.09 \\ 2.87 \end{bmatrix}$

   $= 3.55$ N s at 126° to the initial velocity

3 (a) Work done $= 5 \times 4 \times \cos 60° = 10$ J

   (b) Work done $= 5 \times 4 \times \cos 120° = -10$ J

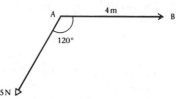

4 (a) Scalar product $= 8 \times 3 \times \cos 64° = 10.5$

   (b) Scalar product $= -16.3$

   (c) Scalar product $= -16.3$

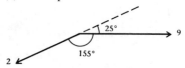

5 (a) Work done $= 100 \cos 20° \times 7 = 660$ J

   (b) Work done $= 660$ J

6 Approximately 190 kJ

   Notice in your working that the mass of the barge is irrelevant (as long as its speed is constant).

7 (a) $\mathbf{F} \cdot \mathbf{r} = 24 - 16 = 8$ J

   (b) $\mathbf{F} \cdot \mathbf{r} = -3 - 8 = -11$ J

8 Force $= \begin{bmatrix} 3 \\ -5 \end{bmatrix}$, displacement $= \begin{bmatrix} 5a \\ 12a \end{bmatrix}$

   $\implies 90 = \begin{bmatrix} 3 \\ -5 \end{bmatrix} \cdot \begin{bmatrix} 5a \\ 12a \end{bmatrix} = 15a - 60a$

   $\implies 90 = -45a$

   $\implies a = -2$

   The displacement is $\begin{bmatrix} -10 \\ -24 \end{bmatrix}$ and the distance travelled is 26 metres.

9 Resultant $= \begin{bmatrix} 12 \\ 12 \end{bmatrix}$, displacement $= \begin{bmatrix} 12a \\ 12a \end{bmatrix}$

   $120 = 144a + 144a \implies a = \tfrac{5}{12}$

   The displacement is $\begin{bmatrix} 5 \\ 5 \end{bmatrix}$ metres.

10 Impulse $= \begin{bmatrix} 0.04 \\ -0.36 \end{bmatrix}$ N s

Initial KE $= \frac{1}{2} \times 0.01 \times (4^2 + 16^2)$

$= 1.36$ J

Final KE $= 2.32$ J

Work done $= 0.96$ J

11 (a) $\mathbf{r} = \begin{bmatrix} 3 \\ 4 \end{bmatrix}$; $\mathbf{F} \cdot \mathbf{r} = 18 + 20 = 38$ J

(b) $0.1v^2 = 38 \implies v = 19.5$ m s^{-1}

B Variable forces (p. 82)

Exercise B (p. 85)

1 (a) $\begin{bmatrix} -9 \\ 9 \end{bmatrix}$ (b) $\begin{bmatrix} 1 \\ 1 \end{bmatrix}$ (c) $\begin{bmatrix} e-1 \\ \frac{1}{2} \end{bmatrix}$

The square bracket notation associated with integration can be used if the vectors are expressed in the **i**, **j** form, e.g. in (a)

$$\int_0^3 \mathbf{F} \, dt = \left[-t^2 \mathbf{i} + 3t\mathbf{j} \right]_0^3$$

$$= -9\mathbf{i} + 9\mathbf{j}$$

2 $10\mathbf{v} - \begin{bmatrix} 10 \\ 30 \end{bmatrix} = \begin{bmatrix} 5t^2 \\ 2t^3 \end{bmatrix}$

$$\implies \mathbf{F} \cdot \mathbf{v} = \begin{bmatrix} 10t \\ 6t^2 \end{bmatrix} \cdot \begin{bmatrix} 5t^2 + 10 \\ 2t^3 + 30 \end{bmatrix} \div 10$$

$$= (50t^3 + 100t + 12t^5 + 180t^2) \div 10$$

$$= 10t + 18t^2 + 5t^3 + 1.2t^5$$

Change in KE $= \left[5t^2 + 6t^3 + 1.25t^4 + 0.2t^6 \right]_0^2$

$$= 20 + 48 + 20 + 12.8$$

$$= 100.8 \text{ units}$$

3 (a) $\mathbf{r} = \begin{bmatrix} 0.84 \\ 0.55 \end{bmatrix}$, $\mathbf{v} = \begin{bmatrix} 0.54 \\ -0.50 \end{bmatrix}$, $\mathbf{a} = \begin{bmatrix} -0.84 \\ -2.2 \end{bmatrix}$

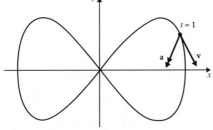

The car is going round the right-hand loop clockwise. At the instant when $t = 1$, the path is curving to the right and the car is speeding up.

(b) Impulse = change in momentum

$$= 0.05 \left(\begin{bmatrix} 0.54 \\ -0.50 \end{bmatrix} - \begin{bmatrix} 1 \\ 1.2 \end{bmatrix} \right)$$

$$= \begin{bmatrix} -0.023 \\ -0.085 \end{bmatrix} \text{N s}$$

Work done = change of KE

$$= \frac{1}{2} \times 0.05 \times (0.54^2 + 0.50^2 - 1^2 - 1.2^2)$$

$$= -0.047 \text{ J}$$

4 (a) $\mathbf{v} = \begin{bmatrix} e^t \\ -e^{-t} \end{bmatrix}$, $\mathbf{a} = \begin{bmatrix} e^t \\ e^{-t} \end{bmatrix}$, $\mathbf{F} = \begin{bmatrix} 2e^t \\ 2e^{-t} \end{bmatrix}$

Impulse $= \int_0^1 \mathbf{F} \, dt = m\mathbf{v} - m\mathbf{u}$

$$= \begin{bmatrix} 2e - 2 \\ -2e^{-1} + 2 \end{bmatrix}$$

Work done $= \int_0^1 \mathbf{F} \cdot \mathbf{v} \, dt = \frac{1}{2}mv^2 - \frac{1}{2}mu^2$

$$= e^2 + e^{-2} - 2$$

(b) $\mathbf{v} = 3 \cos t\mathbf{i} - 5 \sin t\mathbf{j}$

$\mathbf{a} = -3 \sin t\mathbf{i} - 5 \cos t\mathbf{j}$

$\mathbf{F} = -15 \sin t\mathbf{i} - 25 \cos t\mathbf{j}$

Impulse $= -6.9\mathbf{i} - 21.0\mathbf{j}$

WD $= 28.3$

(c) $\mathbf{v} = 2(t+1)\mathbf{i} + 2(t-1)\mathbf{j}$

$\mathbf{a} = 2\mathbf{i} + 2\mathbf{j}$

$\mathbf{F} = 8\mathbf{i} + 8\mathbf{j}$

Impulse $= 8\mathbf{i} + 8\mathbf{j}$

WD $= 16$

5 Write $\mathbf{a} = a_1\mathbf{i} + a_2\mathbf{j}$ and $\mathbf{b} = b_1\mathbf{i} + b_2\mathbf{j}$. Then $\mathbf{a} \cdot \mathbf{b} = a_1 b_1 + a_2 b_2$,

$$\frac{d}{dt}(\mathbf{a} \cdot \mathbf{b}) = \frac{da_1}{dt} b_1 + a_1 \frac{db_1}{dt} + \frac{da_2}{dt} b_2$$

$$+ a_2 \frac{db_2}{dt}$$

$$= \left(\frac{da_1}{dt}\mathbf{i} + \frac{da_2}{dt}\mathbf{j} \right) \cdot (b_1\mathbf{i} + b_2\mathbf{j})$$

$$+ (a_1\mathbf{i} + a_2\mathbf{j}) \cdot \left(\frac{db_1}{dt}\mathbf{i} + \frac{db_2}{dt}\mathbf{j} \right)$$

$$= \frac{d\mathbf{a}}{dt} \cdot \mathbf{b} + \mathbf{a} \cdot \frac{d\mathbf{b}}{dt}$$

Hence $\dfrac{d}{dt} \left(\frac{1}{2}m\mathbf{v} \cdot \mathbf{v} \right) = \frac{1}{2}m(\mathbf{v} \cdot \mathbf{a} + \mathbf{a} \cdot \mathbf{v})$

$$= m\mathbf{a} \cdot \mathbf{v}$$

$$= \mathbf{F} \cdot \mathbf{v}$$

Index

angular acceleration, 23–5, 29–30, 61, 65, 67
angular speed, 20–3, 30, 60–2, 65

centre of mass, 38–43, 46
  applications of, 43–6
  L-shaped lamina, 43–4
  system of particles in a plane, 40–3
  uniform body, 38–9
circular motion in a vertical plane, 64–7
conical pendulum, 60–3, 67
conservation of energy, principle of,
  6–11, 64, 67, 69

elastic potential energy, 57–9, 68–72, 77
energy, 12–19, 68–77
energy laws, 64–7

force, use of assumptions, 2, 8, 10, 24
force laws, 60–7
force/displacement equation, 51–2, 59
force/displacement graph, 51–2, 59
force/time equation, 49–51
force/time graph, 48–51, 59

gravitational potential energy, 5–6, 11,
  68, 77

Hooke's law, 55–9, 69

impact
  particle with a plane surface, 18–19,
    47–8
  two particles, 12–14, 19, 47
impulse, 18, 47–51, 59, 78, 82–3, 85–6

kinetic energy, 1–4, 11–14, 19, 52, 68, 77

modelling, 24, 32, 60–7
moments of a system, 31–4, 36, 38, 46
motion in a horizontal circle, 60–3, 67

Newton's law of gravitation, 26–30
Newton's law of restitution, 16–19
Newton's second law in two dimensions,
  52–3, 67, 78

perfectly elastic, 14–16, 19
perfectly inelastic, 16, 19
potential energy, 4–7, 11
power, 75–7
  for constant force, 83–6

scalar product
  power as, 83–6
  work as, 79–81

work
  done by constant force, 1–3, 51–2,
    79–82, 86
  done by variable force, 51–4, 83–6
  done in stretching an elastic string or
    spring, 57–9
work–energy equation, 2–3, 11, 72–5